SpringerBriefs in Criminology

SpringerBriefs in Criminology present concise summaries of cutting edge research across the fields of Criminology and Criminal Justice. It publishes small but impactful volumes of between 50-125 pages, with a clearly defined focus. The series covers a broad range of Criminology research from experimental design and methods, to brief reports and regional studies, to policy-related applications.

The scope of the series spans the whole field of Criminology and Criminal Justice, with an aim to be on the leading edge and continue to advance research. The series will be international and cross-disciplinary, including a broad array of topics, including juvenile delinquency, policing, crime prevention, terrorism research, crime and place, quantitative methods, experimental research in criminology, research design and analysis, forensic science, crime prevention, victimology, criminal justice systems, psychology of law, and explanations for criminal behavior.

SpringerBriefs in Criminology will be of interest to a broad range of researchers and practitioners working in Criminology and Criminal Justice Research and in related academic fields such as Sociology, Psychology, Public Health, Economics and Political Science.

Dongdong Li • Chi Meng Chu
David P. Farrington
Editors

Emotional and Behavioural Problems of Young Offenders in Singapore

Findings from the EPYC Study

Springer

Editors
Dongdong Li
Translational Social Research Division
National Council of Social Service
Singapore, Singapore

Chi Meng Chu
Ministry of Social and Family Development
National Council of Social Service
Singapore, Singapore

David P. Farrington
Institute of Criminology
University of Cambridge
Cambridge, UK

ISSN 2192-8533 ISSN 2192-8541 (electronic)
SpringerBriefs in Criminology
ISBN 978-3-031-41701-6 ISBN 978-3-031-41702-3 (eBook)
https://doi.org/10.1007/978-3-031-41702-3

This Springer imprint is published by the registered company Springer Nature Switzerland AG
The registered company address is: Gewerbestrasse 11, 6330 Cham, Switzerland

Paper in this product is recyclable.

Preface

This book presents the first results of a prospective longitudinal study, *Enhancing Positive outcomes in Youth and the Community* (EPYC). The study was initiated in Singapore back in 2015 and sought to delve deep into the well-being of young offenders, and advance knowledge about their development into adulthood. In an era when the well-being of children and adolescents has emerged as a paramount concern, this study set out to provide insights about this vulnerable population that is frequently overlooked.

What makes this study truly remarkable is its unique focus on an Asian sample. While research on young offenders has been conducted worldwide, studies examining the issue of Emotional and Behavioural Problems (EBPs) through an Asian lens remain scarce. By examining the experiences of these youths within an Asian context, this study breaks new ground in understanding the complex interplay between risk factors, protective factors, criminal behaviours, and EBP outcomes.

Our team embarked on this ambitious project with a shared understanding that EBP is a crucial topic for designing effective interventions and support systems. By conducting yearly interviews of three cohorts with more than 1000 young offenders, we sought to unravel the underlying factors that contribute to their challenges and, more importantly, to explore the pathways towards resilience and desistance. The findings presented within this book also demonstrate the power of longitudinal research. They offer unique insights into the factors that shape the trajectories of these individuals and provide guidance on the potential strategies for prevention, intervention, rehabilitation, and reintegration.

Publication of these first findings from EPYC is only the start of an important scientific and translational endeavour. Equipped with the vast potential of longitudinal data, we will continue to contribute to the welfare of young individuals who are at the point of overcoming adversity and seizing new opportunities. We hope that this book, as well as future publications, will open up dialogues and inspire changes on how we can better support the young people, their families, and the broader community.

Singapore, Singapore
Dongdong Li
Chi Meng Chu

Cambridge, UK
David P. Farrington

Acknowledgements

The EPYC study is the result of several years of diligent effort and commitment by the project team since 2015. This book is but one of the many fruits from the EPYC study. Without the invaluable contributions of all who have supported us in various capacities, this book would not have been possible. Hence, we extend our heartfelt appreciation to everyone who has played a pivotal role in bringing the EPYC study and this book to fruition.

First, we thank Mr Masagos Zulkifli, Minister for Social and Family Development (the then chair of the National Committee on Prevention, Rehabilitation and Recidivism), for his unwavering support toward EPYC since its inception. His belief and guidance have been instrumental in ensuring the success of the project. We are confident that the EPYC study will contribute significantly toward the vision he has charted for the sector, which is to build a credible body of knowledge and evidence as the foundation for the rehabilitation of youth offenders in Singapore. We also thank Mr Lee Kim Hua and Mr Yoganathan Ammayappan for their pivotal support for this study.

Next, we wish to thank the National Committee on Prevention, Rehabilitation and Recidivism (NCPR), Ministry of Home Affairs (MHA), Ministry of Education (MOE), Ministry of Health (MOH), Family Justice Courts, State Courts of Singapore, Ministry of Finance (MOF), Ministry of Social and Family Development (MSF), National Council of Social Service (NCSS), and National University of Singapore (NUS) for their support of the EPYC study. Their contribution of ideas, time, effort, and manpower have been crucial in the success of the EPYC study and this book. We are deeply grateful for this partnership which have enabled us to advance our understanding of youth offending and rehabilitation in Singapore.

Many colleagues have contributed to the EPYC study over the years. We are especially grateful to Gerald Zeng and Priscilla Koh for their immense assistance in the initial stages of this study. Many thanks to our colleagues from the Rehabilitation and Protection Group at MSF, Central Narcotics Bureau, and Singapore Prison Service. Additionally, the Social Service Research Centre (SSR) at NUS has provided invaluable support throughout the years. We thank Irene Ng for her partnership and assistance as Director, SSR. In the data collection and fieldwork management for this study, Sze Qian Chan, Kala Ruby, and Grace Chng have provided much needed help in training and supporting the fieldwork officers. We are also greatly appreciative for the contributions from Nyx Ng, Nandini Anant, Aaron Lim, Cindy Leow, Yen Cong Wong, Kelly Ng, Yap Xin Yi, Jonathan Liew, and Delia Chia in various areas of the project.

Finally, we wish to highlight that the views expressed here are those of the authors and editors only. They do not represent the official position or policies of the National Council of Social Service or the Ministry of Social and Family Development.

Contents

About the Editors

Dongdong Li is the Principal Research Specialist at the Translational Social Research Division, the National Council of Social Service (NCSS) in Singapore. Her research involves the study of child protection issues and young offender rehabilitation, such as the predictors and outcomes of involvement in child protection services, effects of childhood maltreatment, and the cycle of violence. She has extensive experience in research activities in both academic and government settings in Singapore. She played an instrumental role in several longitudinal studies and has contributed extensively to many international journals, books, and government publications.

Chi Meng Chu is a clinical and forensic psychologist by training, and a registered psychologist with the Singapore Register of Psychologists and also the Australian Health and Practitioner Regulation Agency. In addition, he is registered with the British Psychological Society as a Chartered Psychologist, Chartered Scientist, and Associate Fellow. Presently, Chi Meng is the Director and the Senior Principal Clinical and Forensic Psychologist at the Translational Social Research Division, the National Council of Social Service (NCSS) in Singapore. He is concurrently the Director of Strategic Planning Office at NCSS and also the Director (Special Projects) at the Ministry of Social and Family Development (MSF). Chi Meng currently oversees several large longitudinal and multi-birth-cohort studies in Singapore. Chi Meng also had previous stints in forensic mental health and policy settings.

David P. Farrington, O.B.E., is an Emeritus Professor of Psychological Criminology at Cambridge University. He has received the Stockholm Prize in Criminology, and he has been President of the American Society of Criminology. His major research interest is in developmental criminology, and he is co-Director of the Cambridge Study in Delinquent Development, which is a prospective longitudinal survey of over 400 London males from age 8 to age 61. In addition to 920 published journal articles and book chapters on criminological and psychological topics, he has published 134 books, monographs, and government publications, and 164 shorter publications (total = 1218).

Contributors

Adam Oei is currently the Senior Assistant Director and Lead Research Specialist overseeing research in children in state care. His research interests are in examining early life experiences and later life outcomes such as mental health problems, cognition, and behaviour. He is also interested in examining the interface between biology and the environment and how this shapes human behaviour and cognition.

Eric Hoo is the Principal Clinical Psychologist and Deputy Director of the Translational Social Research Division (TSRD) within the National Council of Social Service (NCSS). He has a keen interest in youth offending and began his career as a practicing psychologist conducting forensic assessments and interventions. Eric was instrumental in the implementation of an evidence-based family intervention, Functional Family Therapy (FFT), in Singapore. Currently overseeing research strategy and engagement, as well as longitudinal studies, he is also interested in programme evaluation and effective implementation of intervention programmes across the social service sector.

Carl Yeo is a Research Specialist at the Translational Social Research Division, the National Council of Social Service (NCSS) in Singapore. His research interests are in criminology, drug abuse, and the interaction between individual and social factors in these domains. He has conducted research on desistance from crime in adult offenders and development of a scale measuring drug abuse cognitions. His recent work involves examining drug abuse in young offenders and the impact of mental health problems on re-offending.

Mengru Liu is a Research Specialist at the Translational Social Research Division, the National Council of Social Service (NCSS) in Singapore. Her research interests lie in understanding motivations of social behaviours, and specifically on the personal and social correlates of offending behaviours. Her recent work involves examining how personal competence and social relationship protect young offenders from mental health problems, and how intervention programmes help these youths to achieve more positive outcomes.

Dennis Teo is a Research Specialist at the Translational Social Research Division, National Council of Social Service (NCSS) in Singapore. His research focuses on applying statistical and machine learning models to draw causal inferences from real world, observational data. His current work with the EPYC focuses on understanding the changes that young offenders undergo upon entering the justice system and estimating the effectiveness of intervention programmes aimed to rehabilitate these youths.

Abbreviations

A*STAR	Agency for Science, Technology and Research
ACE	Adverse Childhood Experiences
ACE-IQ	Adverse Childhood Experiences International Questionnaire
ADHD	Attention Deficit/ Hyperactivity Disorder
AIC	Akaike Information Criterion
ASR	Adult Self-Report
AUC	Area Under Receiver Operating Characteristic Curve
BDI	Beck Depression Inventory
BIC	Bayesian Information Criterion
bMAST	Brief Michigan Alcoholism Screening Test
CBT	Cognitive Behavioural Therapy
CC	Cooperation and Communication
CES-D	Centre for Epidemiologic Studies Depression Scale
CFI	Comparative Fit Index
CLPA	Cross-Lagged Panel Analysis
CI	Confidence Interval
CNB	Central Narcotics Bureau
DAST	Drug Abuse Screening Test
DSM	Diagnostic and Statistical Manual of Mental Disorders
EBPs/EBP	Emotional and Behavioural Problems
EPYC	Enhancing Positive Outcomes in Youth and the Community
FAD	McMaster Family Assessment Device
FF	Family Functioning
FFT	Functional Family Therapy
FIML	Full Information Maximum Likelihood
HA	Home Assets
ICC	Intraclass Correlation Coefficient
IPPA	Inventory of Parent and Peer Attachment
IRB	Institutional Review Board
IRR	Interrater Reliability
LGCM	Latent Growth Curve Model

LONGSCAN	Longitudinal Studies on Child Abuse and Neglect
MLR	Robust Maximum Likelihood
MND	Ministry of National Development
MOE	Ministry of Education
MOH	Ministry of Health
MSF	Ministry of Social and Family Development
NEO-FFI-3	Neo Five Factor Inventory 3
PA	Parent Attachment
PCRS	Probation and Community Rehabilitation Service
RA	Research Assistants
RMSEA	Root Mean Square Error of Approximation
ROC	Receiver operating characteristic curve
RYDM	Resilience and Youth Development Module
SE	Self-Efficacy
SD	Standard Deviation
SPS	Singapore Prison Service
TLI	Tucker-Lewis Index
WHO	World Health Organization
WLSMV	Weighted Least Square with Mean and Variable Adjustment
YLS/CMI 2.0	Youth Level of Service/Case Management Inventory 2.0
YRS	Youth Residential Service
YSR	Youth Self-Report

Chapter 1
Introduction

Chi Meng Chu, David P. Farrington, Dongdong Li, and Adam Oei

Contents

Young offenders have a much higher prevalence, comorbidity, and continuity of emotional and behavioural problems (EBPs) in comparison with the general youth population (Abram et al., 2015; Teplin et al., 2021). It was estimated that as many as 80% of young offenders had at least one diagnosable EBP (Collins et al., 2010; Gilbert et al., 2015). From the current longitudinal studies available, EBPs for these youths tend to persist into adulthood (e.g., Abram et al., 2015; Harrington et al., 2005; Teplin et al., 2012). Notably, 52.3% of males and 30.9% of females still suffered from at least one or more psychiatric disorders 15 years post-detention (Teplin et al., 2021). Meta-analyses have also shown that behavioural problems, such as conduct disorders, were among the main risk factors for persistence in crime (Leschied et al., 2008; Assink, et al., 2015). Similarly, emotional problems at a younger age, such as depression and anxiety, were also found to be moderate risk factors for adult offending (Leschied et al., 2008). Importantly, untreated EBPs among offenders increased the risk for later re-offending (Adily et al., 2023;

C. M. Chu
Ministry of Social and Family Development, National Council of Social Service, Singapore, Singapore

D. P. Farrington
Institute of Criminology, Cambridge University, Cambridge, UK

D. Li (✉) · A. Oei
National Council of Social Service, Singapore, Singapore
e-mail: li_dongdong@ncss.gov.sg

D. Li et al. (eds.), *Emotional and Behavioural Problems of Young Offenders in Singapore*, SpringerBriefs in Criminology,
https://doi.org/10.1007/978-3-031-41702-3_1

Albalawi et al., 2019). Offenders who were not diverted into treatment had higher re-offending rates than those who received treatment (Albalawi et al., 2019) Additionally, more frequent mental health service utilisation by offenders was associated with significant reduction in re-offending risk (Adily et al., 2023). Therefore, EBPs among young offenders not only pose a challenge for the juvenile justice system, but also for the larger mental health system and adult justice system as well (Teplin et al., 2002).

Despite the importance of EBPs in the treatment and rehabilitation of young offenders, there is a dearth of longitudinal studies on the role of such vulnerabilities to explain criminal career development (Basto-Pereira & Farrington, 2022). More research is needed to understand the interrelations of different types of EBPs among young offenders, and how they affect the offending trajectories in the long term. Moreover, there is a lack of research about the risk and protective factors for EBPs among these youths. From a practical standpoint, understanding emotional and behavioural issues alongside criminogenic needs such as antisociality would facilitate the delivery of targeted and possibly more effective interventions for young offenders.

There are few large-scale longitudinal studies on young offenders, especially within Asian jurisdictions. Most of the existing longitudinal studies on youth delinquency have primarily examined general youth populations or those at risk, rather than specifically targeting those who have offended. Examples of such studies include the Cambridge Study in Delinquent Development and the Edinburgh Study of Youth Transitions and Crime in the UK, the Dunedin Multidisciplinary Health and Development Study in New Zealand, and the Korea Youth Panel Survey in South Korea. One notable longitudinal study that specifically focuses on young offenders is the Pathways to Desistance study in the United States. This study spanned 7 years and involved multiple locations, following approximately 1,345 young offenders with serious offences between the ages of 14 and 18 years at the time of their offences. The study aimed to track the transition of these youths into adulthood and their journey away from criminal behaviours. By doing so, it aimed to identify the different paths which they can take to disengage from the juvenile justice system and understand the factors that contribute to their desistance. In Asian countries, a few studies have been published on young offenders, such as the works of Miura and Fuchigami (2017), Hung (2020), Wang et al. (2021), and Zhou et al. (2012). However, these studies either had a restricted timeframe for follow-up or relied on small convenient samples. None of these studies had comprehensive data that included both multiple repeated interviews and long-term tracking of outcomes using administrative records on nationally representative samples.

This book presents findings from the *Enhancing Positive outcomes in Youth and the Community* (EPYC) study. EPYC is a ground-breaking nationwide 10-year longitudinal study on young offenders in Singapore. To set the context, Singapore is an independent island-state that has a land area of 730 square kilometres and a resident population (citizens and permanent residents) of about 4.1 million, of which 19.4% are aged 19 years and below (Singapore Department of Statistics, 2023). Crime rates[1] in Singapore are low at 847 cases per 100,000 population due to effective policies and legislation on gun control and drugs, as well as violent and syndicated crimes (Singapore Police Force, 2021). Being a British colony from the early nineteenth century to the mid-twentieth century resulted in Singapore having a legal system that is similar to many other jurisdictions within the Commonwealth. Singapore is also a melting pot of Eastern and Western ideologies and practices due to its history and unique geographical position within Asia. The past 70 years of globalisation have propelled Singapore's rapid development into a trade hub and international meeting point. It is not surprising that global economic powers such as China, the United States, and Japan, as well as neighbours like Malaysia and Indonesia, are major trading partners of Singapore. This meant that the local culture interacted and fused with ideas and practices from across the globe to become something uniquely Singaporean. That said, the Singaporean society remains primarily Asian, with the Asian values of maintaining strong family and community relationships (Lee & Mock, 2005; Mehta, 2007). Specifically, the family is seen as the basic unit of the society, and there are strong policy efforts directed to reinforce this concept and preserve this position (Ministry of Social and Family Development, 2022; Turnbull, 2020).

Conceived in 2015, this longitudinal study focuses on understanding the trajectories of young offenders, their rehabilitation and reintegration processes, the role of their family members and community in this journey, as well as crime prevention efforts. Ultimately, this study seeks to translate such insights to improve policies, practices, and, most importantly, the outcomes of these youths and their families. Data are collected through yearly interviews, external assessments, and linkage of administrative records to provide a comprehensive picture of participants. In addition, a non-offending youth sample is included as a normative comparison sample. Details about the study, including the research design, variables collected from official databases and self-reported interviews, and the sample characteristics, can be found in Chap. 2.

In addition, Chap. 3 shows the prevalence rates of EBPs in young offenders. Specifically, we sought to examine how EBPs differed across a sample of young offenders and a non-offending youth sample from secondary schools. The comorbidity of EBPs was also examined using network analysis. Importantly, depression was found in Chap. 3 to be a powerful predictor linked to many disorders. In-depth analyses were then conducted to examine the trajectories and risk and protective factors of depressive problems in Chap. 4. In Chaps. 5 and 6, we examine two important outcomes for young offenders: drug use and re-offending. Analyses revealed that EBPs predicted subsequent drug use and re-offending. Furthermore, we examine the protective factors against EBPs such as social relationships and personal resilience in Chap. 7. In Chap. 8, the last chapter, we provide an overview of the findings within the unique Singaporean context and provide

[1] Includes crimes against persons, violent/serious property crimes, housebreaking and related crimes, theft and related crimes, commercial crimes, and miscellaneous crimes.

recommendations to criminal justice research and practice in the areas of EBPs. As this study represents one of the first in Asia and one of few across the globe with such in-depth investigations, we believe that it will advance our understanding of youth offending and associated emotional and behavioural issues. We hope that this book will provide useful insights for researchers, policy makers, and practitioners regarding Singaporean youth and their offending behaviours, especially in relation to EBPs.

References

Abram, K. M., Zwecker, N. A., Welty, L. J., Hershfield, J. A., Dulcan, M. K., & Teplin, L. A. (2015). Comorbidity and continuity of psychiatric disorders in youth after detention: A prospective longitudinal study. *JAMA Psychiatry, 72*(1), 84–93. https://doi.org/10.1001/jamapsychiatry.2014.1375

Adily, A., Albalawi, O., Sara, G., Kariminia, A., Wand, H., Allnutt, S., Schofield, P., Greenberg, D., Grant, L., & Butler, T. (2023). Mental health service utilisation and re-offending in offenders with a diagnosis of psychosis receiving non-custodial sentences: A 14-year follow-up study. *The Australian and New Zealand Journal of Psychiatry, 57*(3), 411–422. https://doi.org/10.1177/00048674221098942

Albalawi, O., Chowdhury, N., Wand, H., Allnutt, S., Greenberg, D., Adily, A., Butler, T. (2019). Court diversion for those with psychosis and its impact on re-offending rates: Results from a longitudinal data-linkage study. *BJPsych Open, 5*(1), E9. https://doi.org/10.1192/bjo.2018.71

Assink, M., van der Put, C., Hoeve, M., de Vries, S., Stams, G., & Oort, F. (2015). Risk factors for persistent delinquent behaviour among juveniles: A meta-analytic review. *Clinical Psychology Review, 42*, 47–61. https://doi.org/10.1016/J.Cpr.2015.08.002

Basto-Pereira, M., & Farrington, D. P. (2022). Developmental predictors of offending and persistence in crime: A systematic review of meta-analyses. *Aggression and Violent Behavior, 65*, 101761. https://doi.org/10.1016/j.avb.2022.101761

Collins, O., Vermeiren, R., Vreugdenhil, C., van den Brink, W., Doreleijers, T., & Broekaert, E. (2010). Psychiatric disorders in detained male adolescents: A systematic literature review. *The Canadian Journal of Psychiatry, 55*(4), 255–263. https://doi.org/10.1177/070674371005500409

Gilbert, A. L., Grande, T. L., Hallman, J., & Underwood, L. A. (2015). Screening incarcerated juveniles using the MAYSI-2. *Journal of Correctional Health Care, 21*(1), 35–44. https://doi.org/10.1177/1078345814557788

Harrington, R. C., Kroll, L., Rothwell, J., McCarthy, K., Bradley, D., & Bailey, S. (2005). Psychosocial needs of boys in secure care for serious or persistent offending. *Journal of Child Psychology and Psychiatry, 46*(8), 859–866. https://doi.org/10.1111/j.1469-7610.2004.00388.x

Hung, E. S. (2020). Psychological risk factors of future drug offending among young offenders in Hong Kong-A longitudinal study. *International Journal of Psychological Studies, 12*(4), 1–31.

Lee, E., & Mock, M. R. (2005). Asian Families. An Overview. In M. McGoldrick, J. Giodarno, & N. Garcia-Preto (Eds.), *Ethnicity and family therapy* (3rd ed., pp. 269–289). Guilford Press.

Leschied, A. W., Chiodo, D., Nowicki, E., & Rodger, S. (2008). Childhood predictors of adult criminality: A meta-analysis drawn from the prospective longitudinal literature. *Canadian Journal of Criminology and Criminal Justice, 50*(4), 435–467. https://doi.org/10.3138/Cjccj.50.4.435

Mehta, K. K. (2007). Multigenerational relationships within the Asian family: Qualitative evidence from Singapore. *International Journal of Sociology of the Family, 33*(1), 63–77. https://www.jstor.org/stable/23070763

Ministry of Social and Family Development. (2022). *Closing address by Minister Masagos Zulkifli at the consortium of institutes on family in the Asian region regional symposium & MSF*

Asian family conference (CIFA-AFC 2022) [Speech transcript]. MSF. https://www.msf.gov.sg/media-room/article/Closing-Address-by-Minister-Masagos-Zulkifli-at-the-Consortium-of-Institutes-on-Family-in-the-Asian-Region-Regional-Symposium%2D%2DMSF-Asian-Family-Conference-CIFA-AFC-2022

Miura, H., & Fuchigami, Y. (2017). Impaired executive function in 14-to 16-year-old boys with conduct disorder is related to recidivism: A prospective longitudinal study. *Criminal Behaviour and Mental Health, 27*(2), 136–145.

Singapore Department of Statistics. (2023). *Population and population structure* [Data set]. DOS. https://www.singstat.gov.sg/find-data/search-by-theme/population/population-and-population-structure/latest-data

Singapore Police Force. (2021). *Singapore Police Force annual report 2021*. https://www.police.gov.sg/media-room/publications?filter=9BC92AE1F3FF452D9CECC3D03C7D5BCB

Teplin, L. A., Abram, K. M., McClelland, G. M., Dulcan, M. K., & Mericle, A. A. (2002). Psychiatric disorders in youth in juvenile detention. *Archives of General Psychiatry, 59*(12), 1133–1143. https://doi.org/10.1001/archpsyc.59.12.1133

Teplin, L. A., Welty, L. J., Abram, K. M., Dulcan, M. K., & Washburn, J. J. (2012). Prevalence and persistence of psychiatric disorders in youth after detention: A prospective longitudinal study. *Archives of General Psychiatry, 69*(10), 1031–1043. https://doi.org/10.1001/archgenpsychiatry.2011.2062

Teplin, L. A., Potthoff, L. M., Aaby, D. A., Welty, L. J., Dulcan, M. K., & Abram, K. M. (2021). Prevalence, comorbidity, and continuity of psychiatric disorders in a 15-year longitudinal study of youths involved in the juvenile justice system. *JAMA Pediatrics, 175*(7), e205807. https://doi.org/10.1001/jamapediatrics.2020.5807

Turnbull, C. B. (2020). *A history of modern Singapore, 1819–2005*. NUS Press.

Wang, X., Zhao, J. S., & Zhang, H. (2021). Factors associated with victimization experiences among juveniles detained in a Chinese correctional facility: A longitudinal study. *Criminal Justice and Behavior, 48*(11), 1596–1615.

Zhou, Z., Xiong, H., Jia, R., Yang, G., Guo, T., Meng, Z., et al. (2012). The risk behaviors and mental health of detained adolescents: A controlled, prospective longitudinal study. *PLoS One, 7*(5), e37199.

Chapter 2
Methodology of the Longitudinal Study

Mengru Liu, Carl Yeo, Eric Hoo, and Dongdong Li

Contents

This chapter provides an overview of (1) the aims of the *Enhancing Positive outcomes for Youth and the Community* (EPYC) study, (2) the baseline and longitudinal samples, (3) data collection procedures, (4) measurement of the variables used, and (5) the data analysis plan. The study received ethical approval from the Ministry of Social and Family Development's Research Ethics Advisory Panel and the Agency for Science, Technology and Research (A*STAR)'s Institutional Review Board (IRB).

M. Liu (✉) · C. Yeo · E. Hoo · D. Li
National Council of Social Service, Singapore, Singapore
e-mail: liu_mengru@ncss.gov.sg

D. Li et al. (eds.), *Emotional and Behavioural Problems of Young Offenders in Singapore*, SpringerBriefs in Criminology,
https://doi.org/10.1007/978-3-031-41702-3_2

2.1 Aims of the Study

The EPYC study is a longitudinal research programme that focuses on crime prevention, rehabilitation, and reintegration of young offenders in Singapore. The aim of the current book is to understand youth offending and the associated emotional and behavioural problems (EBPs). In the subsequent chapters, we will discuss some important topics such as the prevalence rates and comorbidity of EBPs. By examining the EBP networks, we will identify the central variables in such networks. We will then study the trajectories of these central variables and the associated risk and protective factors. We will also examine how drug use and EBPs are associated, as well as how EBPs predict subsequent re-offending. Finally, we explore some factors that would potentially improve EBPs over time. The findings will provide the international community with insights from an Asian perspective. They will shed light on factors affecting successful rehabilitation and reintegration of young offenders.

2.2 Sample

2.2.1 Baseline Sample

The baseline sample, which refers to participants in the first wave of data collection, is used in Chap. 3. The EPYC project used a census survey method, targeting every young offender and/or drug user aged between 12 and 19 years in the first year of their court/drug orders between 2016 and 2018 for three consecutive cohorts. Young offenders who met our inclusion criteria were referred to the study from various youth justice agencies such as the Probation and Community Rehabilitation Service (PCRS), Youth Residential Service (YRS), Central Narcotics Bureau (CNB), and Singapore Prison Service (SPS). These youths were included because they were issued orders for probation, residential stay, drug rehabilitation, reformative training, or incarceration. In other words, we sampled from the entire population of young offenders over the 3 years.

Out of the 1,595 eligible young offenders, we obtained written consent from participants and their legal guardians. A total of 1,311 participants consented (82.2% consent rate) and 1,224 of them completed the interview at baseline (93.3% completion rate). The number of participants in each cohort at baseline was 385 for Cohort 1, 405 for Cohort 2, and 434 for Cohort 3. The majority of this offender sample were males (84.6%) and of non-Chinese ethnicity (68.0%). The details of the baseline sample characteristics can be found in Table 2.1.

In addition, we included a comparison sample in 2019, with 655 non-offender youths recruited from ten secondary schools. These schools were referred to us by the Ministry of Education. As this was a convenience sample, no sampling frame

Table 2.1 EPYC baseline sample characteristics

	Offender	Non-offender
Sample size	1,224	655
Sex		
Male	1,035 (84.6%)	340 (51.9%)
Female	189 (15.4%)	315 (48.1%)
Race		
Chinese	392 (32.0%)	420 (64.1%)
Non-Chinese	832 (68.0%)	235 (35.9%)
Age		
Average in years (SD, range)	17.6 (1.55, 12–19)	15.5 (1.27, 11–20)

Table 2.2 EPYC offender sample representativeness

	Respondents	Nonrespondents
Sample size	1,224	371
Sex		
Male	1035 (84.6%)	329 (88.7%)
Female	189 (15.4%)	42 (11.3%)
Race		
Chinese	392 (32.0%)	125 (33.6%)
Non-Chinese	832 (68.0%)	246 (66.3%)
Age		
Average in years (SD, range)	17.6 (1.55, 12–19)	17.6 (1.52, 13–20)

was used. We surveyed all students who provided written consent. Participants were excluded if they lacked a legal guardian or had intellectual disability. The sex proportion of this sample is almost equal with 51.9% males. The majority of the sample was Chinese (64.1%). This sample is similar to the national youth population aged 10–19 years in 2019, with 51% males and 71.5% of Chinese ethnicity (Singapore Department of Statistics, 2022).

2.2.2 *Baseline Sample Representativeness*

In our sample of young offenders, sample representativeness analysis was performed to compare the sex, race, and age distributions for 1,224 respondents and 371 nonrespondents (see Table 2.2). Respondents and nonrespondents were similar in sex, race, and age.

Table 2.3 EPYC longitudinal sample characteristics

	Wave 1	Wave 2	Wave 3
Sample size	790	755	599
Sex			
Male	669 (84.7%)	643 (85.2%)	512 (85.5%)
Female	121 (15.3%)	112 (14.8%)	87 (14.5%)
Race			
Chinese	258 (32.7%)	240 (31.8%)	193 (32.2%)
Non-Chinese	532 (67.3%)	515 (68.2%)	406 (67.8%)
Age at wave 1			
Average in years (SD)	17.6 (1.45)	17.5 (1.45)	17.5 (1.49)

2.2.3 *Longitudinal Sample*

The longitudinal sample is used in Chaps. 4, 5, 6, and 7. Our longitudinal sample consists of 835 young offenders from Cohorts 1 and 2 as they had 3 waves of data available. In this sample, there were 707 males (84.7%) and 128 females (15.3%), while the racial breakdown was 269 Chinese (32.2%) and 566 non-Chinese (67.8%). Participants' age ranged from 12 to 19, with the mean age of 17.6 years ($SD = 1.44$, median = 17.8).

In each wave, we contacted all consenting participants for interviews unless they withdrew their consent. Some participants only agreed to participate after Wave 1 was completed, so they started in later waves. Wave-to-wave retention rates (*n* youth who completed the current wave/*n* youth who completed the previous wave) were 95.6% and 79.3%, respectively. In total, 543 youths completed all three waves, and 766 completed at least two waves. The descriptive statistics of the sample at each wave are shown in Table 2.3.

2.3 Data Collection Procedures

Data for the study were obtained from three sources: questionnaires, case file coding, and administrative records. The questionnaires were administered by trained fieldwork research assistants (RA) through face-to-face structured interviews with youth respondents. Participants self-reported their EBPs, personality, childhood experiences, personal competence, family relationship, substance use, and so forth. The interviews were conducted annually with an average duration of 150 minutes. Young offenders were approached for the first interview within 90 days of their date of conviction. The subsequent annual interviews were scheduled around 9–15 months after the preceding interview completion date and before the wave closing date of May each year. Case file coding was done by RAs within 2 weeks of the youth questionnaire interview to assess protective factors and factors related to criminogenic needs. Criminogenic needs refer to factors directly related to offending, such as antisocial personality, criminal attitudes, dysfunctional family relations, antisocial peers, and substance use (Andrews et al., 2006). Data were coded based on the interviews and case files provided by the youth justice agencies. Finally, administrative data were retrieved from collaborating agencies (i.e., Ministry of Health, Singapore Prison Service) and linked with the questionnaire and coding data. Examples of data include health records, education history, and subsequent re-offences.

For unresponsive participants, RAs exhausted all avenues of contact before declaring participants as uncontactable cases for the current interview wave. Apart from participants' contact numbers, other avenues of contact included caregivers' contact numbers, sending a letter to participants' homes, and visiting participants' homes. When participants were unresponsive for three waves, they were deemed to be withdrawn and were not contacted anymore.

Participants' confidentiality was ensured throughout the project. Identifiable information (e.g., name, contact number) was stored in a password-protected file and kept separate from questionnaire data. Only members of the fieldwork team had access to the identifiable information for arranging interviews. The questionnaire data contained no identifiable information, and access was restricted to members of the analysis team only. This ensured that participants' questionnaire data stored with the analysis team would not be linked with identifiable information stored with the fieldwork team. As an additional measure to protect confidentiality and facilitate tracking across interview waves, each participant was assigned a serial number to be used throughout the study and was the primary means of referring to participants. Finally, data analyses used only de-identified data.

2.4 Measures

Participants' sex, race, and date of birth were obtained in the demographics section of the questionnaire. Participants' date of birth was used to compute their age in their cohort year. Participants' household dwelling type was based on the linkage data obtained from the Ministry of National Development (MND) in Singapore.

Besides these demographics, the following areas were examined in the study: (1) emotional and behavioural problems (EBPs) as the focus of the analysis; (2) personality and adverse childhood experiences as general risk factors, and the Level of Risk created based on eight major criminogenic needs as a specific risk factor for re-offending; (3) protective assets, family functioning, and parent attachment as protective factors; and (4) drug use and re-offending as indicators of involvement in criminal behaviours. The assessment of these areas is detailed below.

2.4.1 Measures of EBPs

The Youth Self-Report (YSR) and Adult Self-Report (ASR) YSR/ASR were used to measure individuals' self-reported mental health problems along two broad dimensions: emotional and behavioural (Achenbach, 1991). Emotional problems were characterised by distress within the self, such as anxiety, somatisation, and depression, whereas behavioural problems were described as discomfort and conflict towards others in the external world, such as aggressive, oppositional, and delinquent behaviour (Achenbach, 1991; Bongers et al., 2003). The two constructs differ considerably. Delineating them may capture heterogeneous developmental patterns that could inform subsequent intervention designs. The following DSM-oriented scales as shown in Table 2.4 were used in this study:

All participants responded to YSR for the first two waves, while those aged older than 19 years responded to ASR at Wave 3 onwards. To complete YSR/ASR, respondents reported how applicable the items were in reflecting their behaviours, thoughts, and feelings of the previous 6 months, by rating on three-point scales, from *not true (0)*, *somewhat or sometimes true (1)*, to *very true or often true (2)*. Higher scores meant that the respondent was facing more problems. The sum score for each subscale was computed. The sum score was further converted to a *T-score* to create a binary variable for each subscale to identify those who fell within the clinical range. A *T-score* is a normalised score that compares the respondent's score with the distribution of scores in a normative sample of children (Achenbach & Rescorla, 2001). The *T-score* therefore shows how well a respondent is in comparison to a normative sample and also allows comparison between different YSR/ASR scales. Though not diagnostic, these DSM-oriented scales were found to have good

Table 2.4 EBPs measured by YSR/ASR

	Example item	No. of items	Included in…
Emotional problems			
Depression	I am unhappy, sad, or depressed	13	YSR and ASR
Anxiety problems	I worry a lot	9	YSR and ASR
Somatic problems	Physical problems without a known medical cause: Headaches	7	YSR and ASR
Behavioural problems			
Attention-deficit hyperactivity disorder (ADHD)	I am inattentive or easily distracted	7	YSR and ASR
Oppositional problems	I disobey at school	5	YSR
Conduct problems	I steal from places other than home	15	YSR
Antisocial personality problems	I argue a lot	20	ASR

psychometric properties (Nakamura et al., 2009) and hence were used as the measurement of EBPs in all chapters.

Substance Dependence Besides those measured by YSR/ASR, substance dependence was used as an additional behavioural problem in Chaps. 3 and 6. It is a composite variable created by combining the brief Michigan Alcoholism Screening Test (bMAST; Pokorny et al., 1972) and the Drug Abuse Screening Test (DAST; Skinner, 1982). DAST and bMAST both comprise ten items. The bMAST provides a quick assessment of alcoholism (e.g., "Have you ever gone to anyone for help about your drinking?"), whereas DAST focuses on respondents' drug abuse problems (e.g., "Do you abuse more than one drug at a time?") in the past 12 months, excluding alcohol and tobacco use. Respondents were asked to indicate yes or no for each item, with a point assigned to each yes, except for the reverse-coded items. Participants were coded as having substance dependence if they scored 6 or more on the DAST or scored 5 or more on the bMAST.

Health Records In addition to the self-report measures, participants' physical and mental health records, based on administrative data, were obtained from the Ministry of Health (MOH) of Singapore. Data from these records are used in Chaps. 3 and 4. Chapter 3 uses the official records of participants who received a mental disorder diagnosis from a public health institution, whereas Chap. 4 uses the number of visits to health institutions due to physical or mental health conditions.

2.4.2 *Measures of Risk Factors*

Neuroticism The NEO Five Factor Inventory 3 (NEO-FFI-3; McCrae & Costa, 2010) was used to measure neuroticism (e.g., "I often feel tense and jittery."), one of the Big Five dimensions of personality. Neuroticism refers to the general tendency to experience negative affect (McCrae & Costa, 2010). It includes 12 items, with each item rated on a 5-point scale ranging from *strongly disagree (0)* to *strongly agree (4)*. Mean scores were computed to obtain respondents' scores for neuroticism. Higher scores imply that the respondent exhibits more traits characteristic of neuroticism. The NEO-FFI-3 Neuroticism subscale was used in Chap. 4.

Adverse Childhood Experiences The Adverse Childhood Experiences International Questionnaire (ACE-IQ) from the World Health Organization (WHO, 2012) was used to measure adverse childhood experiences. We used 27 items to assess the following 12 categories of adverse childhood experiences as shown in Table 2.5. Items measuring the first four categories were rated on binary *(yes or no)* scales, and the other items for the remaining categories were rated on a four-point scale, ranging from *never (0)* to *many times (3)*. If any component item of a certain category was above the specific frequency following guidelines stipulated in the ACE-IQ manual, the category's score was coded as "1" (yes). For instance, according to the manual, a respondent is considered physically abused only if he or she was slapped many times. The details are summarised in Table 2.5. ACE-IQ is used in Chap. 4.

Level of Re-offending Risk The Youth Level of Service/Case Management Inventory 2.0 (YLS/CMI 2.0) was used to measure youth's re-offending risk level (Hodge & Andrews, 2011). There was a total of 42 risk items used in 8 subscales: (1) prior and current offences/dispositions, (2) family circumstances/parenting, (3) education/employment, (4) peer relations, (5) substance abuse, (6) leisure/recreation, (7) personality/behaviour, and (8) attitudes/orientation. The major criminogenic needs from eight domains were summed into a total score and categorised into three risk levels: Low-Rrisk, Moderate-Risk, and High-Risk. We merged the YLS/

Table 2.5 Adverse Childhood Experiences International Questionnaire (ACE-IQ)

Categories	Example item	No. of items	Coded "Yes" (1) if…
Household substance abuse	Did you live with a household member who was a problematic drinker, an alcoholic, misused drugs, or prescription drugs?	1	If answered "yes"
Household mental illness	Did you live with a household member who was depressed, mentally ill, or suicidal?	1	If answered "yes"
Household incarceration	Did you live with a household member who was ever sent to jail or prison?	1	If answered "yes"
Parental separation	Were your parents ever separated or divorced?	2	If answered "yes"
Emotional abuse	Did a parent, guardian or other household member yell, scream, or swear at you, insult or humiliate you?	2	If answered "many times" to either
Physical abuse	Did a parent, guardian, or other household member spank, slap, kick, punch, or beat you up?	2	If answered "many times" to either
Sexual abuse	Did someone touch or fondle you in a sexual way when you did not want them to?	4	If answered "once" and above to any
Home violence	Did you see or hear a parent or household member in your home being yelled at, screamed at, sworn at, insulted, or humiliated?	3	If answered "few times or many times" to any
Emotional neglect	Did your parents/guardians understand your problems and worries?	2	If answered "never" or "once" to either
Physical neglect	How often did your parents/guardians not give you enough food even when they could easily have done so?	3	If answered "many times" to any
Peer victimisation	How often were you bullied?	1	If answered "many times"
Community violence	Did you see or hear someone being stabbed or shot in real life?	3	If answered "many times" to any

CMI Very-High-Risk category into the High-Risk category as there were very few participants with Very-High-Risk.

The YLS/CMI 2.0 was coded by our interviewers based on the interviews and other administrative data. Interrater reliability (IRR) was measured by a one-way random effect intraclass correlation coefficient (ICC) model. Based on Koo and Li (2016) guidelines, the coding on YLS/CMI 2.0 had moderate to good interrater reliability for each subscale and the total score (ICC: 0.53–0.89). Additionally, the YLS/CMI 2.0 showed good predictive validity for actual re-offending rates overseas (Basto-Pereira et al., 2021) and in Singapore (Chu et al., 2015, 2020). The YLS/CMI 2.0 was used in Chap. 6.

2.4.3 Measures of Protective Factors

Protective Assets The Resilience and Youth Development Module (RYDM) was used to assess the external and internal protective factors, which was adapted from the California Healthy Kids Survey (Constantine & Benard, 2001). The RYDM measures both internal and external assets. External protective assets refer to the meaningful and prosocial bonding that respondents have with their families, communities, schools, and peers, whereas internal assets refer to the personal strength and individual qualities associated with successful outcomes (Constantine & Benard, 2001). The items are summarised in Table 2.6. Each item was rated on a four-point scale ranging from *not at all true (1)* to *very much true (4)*. Higher scores imply that the respondent has more protective assets. The RYDM was used in Chaps. 4 and 7.

Family Functioning The McMaster Family Assessment Device (FAD) assesses general family functioning (Epstein et al., 1978, 1983). The instrument comprises 12 items (e.g., "We can express feelings to each other."). Respondents rated all items on four-point scales ranging from *strongly agree (1)* to *strongly disagree (4)*. We reverse-coded the scores and computed the mean scores. Higher scores indicate better family functioning. The FAD was used in Chap. 7.

Parent Attachment The revised Inventory of Parent and Peer Attachment (IPPA; Armsden & Greenberg, 1987) assesses youth's perceptions of their overall attachment with their mothers and fathers. Measures of each attachment figure comprises 25 items (e.g., "My mother respects my feelings.") rated on a five-point scale, from *almost never or never true (1)* to *almost always or always true (5)*. The father attachment and the mother attachment were highly correlated and showed non-divergent effects in the analysis, so they were further combined to yield one overall parent attachment score. Higher scores imply higher parent attachment. The IPPA was used in Chap. 7.

Table 2.6 Resilience and Youth Development Module (RYDM)

Protective assets	Example item				No. of items
External	Context	Caring relationship	High expectation	Meaningful participation	
Home	In my home, there is a parent or some other adult…	Who really cares about me	Who tells me when I do a good job	I do interesting activities	9
Peer	I have a friend about my own age…				4
School	At my school, there is a teacher or some other adult…				9
Community	Outside of my home or school, there is an adult…				9
Internal					
Empathy	I try to understand how other people feel and think				3
Problem-solving	When I need help, I find someone to talk with				3
Self-efficacy	I can do most things if I try				3
Self-awareness	There is a purpose to my life				3
Cooperation and communication	I enjoy working together with other students my age				3
Goals and aspirations	I have goals and plans for the future				3

2.4.4 Measures of Criminal Behaviours

Drug Use We investigated respondents' drug use behaviour on 19 types of drugs. Some examples include heroin, amphetamine, cocaine, and cannabis. Participants rated their frequency of use of each drug in the past 12 months on a six-point scale, from *never/not used (0)* to *daily use (5)*. Each item was dichotomised into a binary variable for each drug such that participants who scored 0 are recoded as "0" *(no)*, while scores of 1 to 5 are recoded as "1" *(yes)*. Participants with a score of "1" (yes) on any type of drug were considered having used drugs. Measures of drug use were used in Chap. 5.

Re-offending Administrative data was used to calculate re-offending. We measured re-offending as any offence or revocation that resulted in a new sentence within 2 years from the start of their index offence, the offence which led to participation in the EPYC study. Examples of offences include theft, robbery, sexual offending, and drug trafficking. Re-offending is used in Chap. 6.

2.5 Analytical Plan

To achieve the research aims, we performed various statistical analyses to examine the following topics:

Prevalence and Comorbidity of EBPs In Chap. 3, besides descriptive statistics, we examine the co-occurrence among emotional and behavioural problems using network analysis. Network analysis provides a simple graphical representation of complex high-dimensional multivariate relationships (Epskamp et al., 2017), as well as identifying the variable that is considered most important in influencing other variables. In a network model, variables are represented as nodes. The direction and strength of the relationships between nodes are examined after controlling for all other nodes in the network (Cramer et al., 2010; Hevey, 2018; Epskamp et al., 2018).

Trajectory, Risk, and Protective Factors for EBPs Chapters 4 and 7 examine the trajectory of EBPs and protective factors through latent growth curve models (LGCM). LGCMs estimate the intercept and the slope as latent factors to represent the trajectory. The intercept indicates the initial status at baseline, and the slope indicates the rate of change over time. Chapter 4 presents a univariate LGCM on depression to show the average score and its variance at baseline, as well as the change in depression. Robust maximum likelihood (MLR) was used as the estimation method to utilise the full information maximum likelihood (FIML) approach with robust standard errors to deal with missing data. Compared to the listwise/pairwise deletion method or even multiple imputation, this is a preferred method to deal with missing data in longitudinal analyses, providing correct estimates with robust standard errors (Larsen, 2011).

Chapter 7 presents several multivariate LGCMs to evaluate how changes in protective factors affect changes in EBPs. In these models, trajectories for two time-varying variables were estimated simultaneously to examine how the two trajectories were related. The covariance between intercepts of both trajectories represents how the two variables relate to each other at baseline. The path coefficient of the intercept on slope represents how the baseline of one variable affects the rate of change of the other variable, whereas the path coefficient of slope on slope represents how the growth rate of one variable affects how the other variable changes over time.

EBPs and Drug Use To examine how EBPs and drug use influence each other over time, we conduct a cross-lagged panel analysis (CLPA) in Chap. 5. CLPA is a method used to describe the directional influence that variables have on each other over time (Kearney, 2017; Kuiper & Ryan, 2018). Key relationships in CLPA are the cross-lagged relationships and stability relationships. The cross-lagged relationship examines how one variable (A) at baseline affects the other variable (B) at later waves and how the other variable (B) at baseline affects the variable (A) at later waves. Stability relationships examine how the same variable influences itself over time.

EBPs and Re-offending Chapter 6 examines whether EBPs as predictors provide additional predictive power for estimating the probability of re-offending, over and above that explained by the effects of offenders' Level of Risk. We examine this through logistic regression models which are used to estimate the probability or odds of an event occurring given a set of variables. The model's fit indices include likelihood ratio $\chi 2$ (LCRS), Akaike information criterion (AIC), and Bayesian information criterion (BIC). Better models were indicated by a significant likelihood ratio test along with lower AIC and BIC scores. Each model's predictive accuracy was shown by their area under the receiver operating characteristic curve (AUC) with higher AUC values indicating better accuracy. Our findings on re-offending as the outcome are presented using the odds ratio, which is the odds that an event (re-offending) will occur. Odds ratio above 1 indicates higher odds of re-offending while odds ratio below 1 indicates a lower odds of re-offending.

2.6 Summary

The Enhancing Positive outcomes for Youth and the Community (EPYC) study is a nationwide longitudinal study on young offenders in Singapore. It focuses on understanding crime prevention, rehabilitation, and reintegration of these youths. Data are collected through yearly interviews, case file coding, and linkage of administrative records to provide a comprehensive picture of participants. In addition, a non-offender youth sample is included as a normative comparison sample. The data collection and analysis methods as well as the included measures as described in this chapter should be used as reference while reading the subsequent chapters.

References

Achenbach, T. M. (1991). *Manual for the youth self-report and 1991 profile*. Department of Psychiatry, University of Vermont.

Achenbach, T. M., & Rescorla, L. A. (2001). *Manual for ASEBA school-age forms & profiles*. University of Vermont, Research Center for Children, Youth & Families.

Andrews, D. A., Bonta, J., & Wormith, J. S. (2006). The recent past and near future of risk and/or need assessment. *Crime & Delinquency, 52*(1), 7–27. https://doi.org/10.1177/0011128705281756

Armsden, G. C., & Greenberg, M. T. (1987). The inventory of parent and peer attachment: Individual differences and their relationship to psychological Well-being in adolescence. *Journal of Youth and Adolescence, 16*(5), 427–454. https://doi.org/10.1007/BF02202939

Basto-Pereira, M., Villanueva, L., Peterson-Badali, M., Pimentel, A., Quintas, J., Cuervo, K., Hoge, R. D., & Skilling, T. A. (2021). Is a 7-item combination from the YLS/CMI an effective screening strategy for risk to reoffend? Findings from a cross-national study. *Criminal Justice and Behavior, 48*(5), 655–670. https://doi.org/10.1177/0093854821995866

Bongers, I. L., Koot, H. M., van der Ende, J., & Verhulst, F. C. (2003). The normative development of child and adolescent problem behavior. *Journal of Abnormal Psychology, 112*(2), 179. https://doi.org/10.1037/0021-843x.112.2.179

Chu, C. M., Lee, Y., Zeng, G., Yim, G., Tan, C. Y., Ang, Y., Chin, S., & Ruby, K. (2015). Assessing youth offenders in a non-Western context: The predictive validity of the YLS/CMI ratings. *Psychological Assessment, 27*(3), 1013–1021. https://doi.org/10.1037/a0038670

Chu, C. M., Xu, X., Li, D., Ruby, K., & Chng, G. S. (2020). The utility of SAPROF-YV ratings for predicting recidivism in male youth under community supervision in Singapore. *Criminal Justice and Behavior, 47*(11), 1409–1427. https://doi.org/10.1177/0093854820949595

Constantine, N. A., & Benard, B. (2001). California healthy kids survey resilience assessment module: Technical report. *Journal of Adolescent Health, 28*(2), 122–140. Retrieved from http://crahd.phi.org/projects/welcome.html

Cramer, A. O. J., Waldorp, L. J., Maas, H. L. J., van der Maas, H. J. J., & Borsboom, D. (2010). Comorbidity: A network analysis. *Behavioral and Brain Sciences, 33*(2–3), 137–150. https://doi.org/10.1017/s0140525x09991567

Epskamp, S., Kruis, J., & Marsman, M. (2017). Estimating psychopathological networks: Be careful what you wish for. *PLoS One, 12*(6), e0179891. https://doi.org/10.1371/journal.pone.0179891

Epskamp, S., Borsboom, D., & Fried, E. I. (2018). Estimating psychological networks and their accuracy: A tutorial paper. *Behavior Research Methods, 50*(1), 195–212. https://doi.org/10.3758/s13428-017-0862-1

Epstein, N. B., Bishop, D. S., & Levin, S. (1978). The McMaster model of family functioning. *Journal of Marriage and Family Counselling, 4*(4), 19–31. https://doi.org/10.1111/j.1752-0606.1978.tb00537.x

Epstein, N. B., Baldwin, L. M., & Bishop, D. S. (1983). The McMaster family assessment device. *Journal of Marital and Family Therapy, 9*(2), 171–180.

Hevey, D. (2018). Network analysis: A brief overview and tutorial. *Health Psychology and Behavioral Medicine, 6*(1), 301–328. https://doi.org/10.1080/21642850.2018.1521283

Hodge, R. D., & Andrews, D. A. (2011). *Youth level of service/case management inventory 2.0 (YLS/CMI 2.0): User's manual*. Multi-Health Systems.

Kearney, M. W. (2017). The SAGE Encyclopedia of Communication Research Methods. SAGE Publications. https://doi.org/10.4135/9781483381411

Koo, T. K., & Li, M. Y. (2016). A guideline of selecting and reporting intraclass correlation coefficient for reliability research. *Journal of Chiropractic Medicine, 15*, 155–163. https://doi.org/10.1016/j.jcm.2016.02.012

Kuiper, R. M., & Ryan, O. (2018). Drawing conclusions from cross-lagged relationships: Re-considering the role of the time-interval. *Structural Equation Modeling: A Multidisciplinary Journal, 25(5), 809–823.* https://doi.org/10.1080/10705511.2018.1431046

Larsen, R. (2011). Missing data imputation versus full information maximum likelihood with second-level dependencies. *Structural Equation Modeling: A Multidisciplinary Journal, 18*(4), 649–662.

McCrae, R. R., & Costa, P. T. (2010). *NEO inventories for the NEO personality Inventory-3 (NEO-PI-3), NEO five-factor Inventory-3 (NEO-FFI-3), NEO personality inventory-revised (NEO PI-R): Professional manual*. Psychological Assessment Resources.

Nakamura, B. J., Ebesutani, C., Bernstein, A., & Chorpita, B. F. (2009). A psychometric analysis of the child behavior checklist DSM-oriented scales. *Journal of Psychopathology and Behavioral Assessment, 31, 178–189.*

Pokorny, A. D., Miller, B. A., & Kaplan, H. B. (1972). The brief MAST: A shortened version of the Michigan alcoholism screening test. *American Journal of Psychiatry, 129*(3), 342–345. https://doi.org/10.1176/ajp.129.3.342

Singapore Department of Statistics. (2022). *Singapore residents by age group, ethnic group and sex, end june, annual* [Data Set]. DOS. https://tablebuilder.singstat.gov.sg/table/TS/M810011

Skinner, H. A. (1982). The drug abuse screening test. *Addictive Behaviors, 7*(4), 363–371. https://doi.org/10.1016/0306-4603(82)90005-3

World Health Organisation. (2012). *Adverse childhood experiences international questionnaire (ACE-IQ).* Retrieved from www.who.int/violence_injury_prevention/violence/activities/adverse_childhood_experiences/en/index.html

Chapter 3
Prevalence and Comorbidity of Emotional and Behavioural Problems of Young Offenders in Singapore

Adam Oei

Contents

The link between mental and behavioural disorders and youth offending is well established (Beaudry et al., 2021; Fazel et al., 2008; Hartsell, 2021; Karnik et al., 2009; Livanou et al., 2016; Seena et al., 2008; Underwood & Washington, 2016). As many as 61.7% of young offenders have EBPs compared to 14% of the general population (Beaudry et al., 2021).

A. Oei (✉)
National Council of Social Service, Singapore, Singapore
e-mail: adam_oei@ncss.gov.sg

D. Li et al. (eds.), *Emotional and Behavioural Problems of Young Offenders in Singapore*, SpringerBriefs in Criminology,
https://doi.org/10.1007/978-3-031-41702-3_3

3.1 The Mental Disorder Treatment Gap

The high prevalence rate of mental and behavioural health disorders in young offenders poses significant problems in their rehabilitation. Unfortunately, these problems are often unmet in the general population and also in the offender population. Untreated mental disorders multiply the risk of re-offending among young offenders (Guebert & Olver, 2014; McReynolds et al., 2010; Mulder et al., 2010), and are associated with poorer outcomes later, such as adjustment problems (van der Molen et al., 2013), as well as substance use, and depression problems (Teplin et al., 2012).

The mental disorder "treatment gap" is conceptualised as the proportion of individuals who have mental health conditions, but do not seek help for them (Kohn et al., 2004). The treatment gap in the adult population has been shown in the Singapore Mental Health Study previously (Subramaniam et al., 2020). Specifically, 78.6% of adult participants self-reported having mental health disorders in the preceding 12 months, but had not received any treatment. This gap is comparable with other jurisdictions such as Japan (Ishikawa et al., 2016), Switzerland (Michel et al., 2018), and various parts of the Americas such as the United States, Mexico, Argentina, Brazil, and Canada (Kohn et al., 2018). This problem is especially poignant among youth and adolescents, as adolescent onset mental health disorders may affect neurodevelopment, and the resulting maturational lag may persist well into adulthood (Kaufmann et al., 2017). Childhood and adolescent onset mental health disorders do not go away without treatment, and if left untreated, often result in worse prognosis and outcomes in adulthood (Loeber & Farrington, 2000; Weissman et al., 1999). Therefore, in youth justice systems, it is crucial that these youths are screened for mental disorders through self-report and/or rating scales during intake interviews.

3.2 Co-occurrence of EBPs

Co-occurrence of different EBPs is common (Brown et al., 2001; Kessler et al., 2012; Ottosen et al., 2016). Moreover, the risk of developing another EBP escalates after an index problem (Plana-Ripoll et al., 2018). Individuals with co-occurring problems tend to have poorer prognosis and quality of life relative to those with single conditions (Bhalla et al., 2018; Sherbourne & Wells, 1997; Zhou et al., 2017). Additionally, each EBP may have its own progression, which in turn complicates treatment. Recent findings have also shown a high prevalence of psychiatric comorbidities among offenders (Kim et al., 2017), where the presence of comorbidities was in turn associated with higher re-offending rates. These add on an additional layer of complexity in the rehabilitation of offenders.

3.3 Examining EBP Comorbidity Using Network Analyses

There has been a surge of interest in using network models to examine the co-occurrence of mental disorders (Borsboom & Cramer, 2013; Cramer et al., 2010). Examples of these include network structures of depressive symptoms in low-income mothers (Santos et al., 2018), psychopathology in community preadolescents (Boschloo et al., 2016), and international adoptees (Elovainio et al., 2018). More recently, network approaches have also been utilised by researchers on youth offending samples examining network structure for psychopathy, as well as dynamic risk factors in risk assessment tools for sexual re-offending (McCuish et al., 2019; van den Berg et al., 2020). However, to date, there is a lack of studies that have examined the comorbidity of mental disorders in young offenders.

A network model consists of variables represented as nodes, while edges represent statistical relationships between nodes that can be estimated from the data (Cramer et al., 2010; Hevey, 2018). These edges are typically depicted in varying thicknesses to show the strength of the relationship, and are coloured red or green/blue depending on whether the relationships between nodes are negative or positive, respectively. A network thus depicts the strength of the relationships between nodes after controlling for all other nodes in the network (Epskamp et al., 2018). Additionally, researchers commonly produce centrality indices to show which node is the most central or "important" in the network. Relative "importance" indicates how well a node is interconnected to other nodes in the network. There are a few "centrality" measures typically produced in network analyses. It has been argued, however, that node strength centrality, which is the sum of the absolute value of the edge weights (correlation), is the most important metric for psychopathology relative to other metrics (McNally, 2020). Put simply, it indicates the strength of the correlations between a particular node and others that are connected to it in the network.

A virtue of the network model is that it allows a simple graphical representation of complex high dimensional multivariate relationships between mental disorders (Epskamp et al., 2017). This allows for better representation of psychopathology as a set of interconnected symptoms, rather than as separate entities (Borsboom & Cramer, 2013).

3.4 The Current Study

This chapter aims to set the context and background for the following chapters in this book by providing data on the prevalence on various EBPs and substance dependency. We used the Youth Self Report (YSR; Achenbach, 2001), and self-reported substance dependence from the brief Michigan Alcohol Screening Test (bMAST; Pokorny et al., 1972), and Drug Abuse Screening Test (DAST; Skinner, 1982) to explore how EBPs and substance dependency co-occur in different subgroups. Our presentation of a network enables practitioners to comprehensively understand the mental and behavioural problem profiles of young offenders and their comorbidity. Through this, practitioners can target intervention to different problems and assess their potential impact on others. Practitioners can also divert their limited resources towards the problems that are best connected to others to gain maximal impact. Here, we present the networks of young offenders and non-offenders. Additionally, as the prevalence of EBPs also differ between sexes (Cauffman et al., 2007; Stewart et al., 2020; Wasserman et al., 2005), we also present network findings for male and female offenders for comparison. Finally, this chapter will present statistics on the "treatment gap" for both offender and non-offender samples to underscore the importance of comprehensive screening for EBPs in the general population and youth justice systems.

3.5 Prevalence of Self-Reported EBPs

3.5.1 Comparison Between Young Offender and Non-offender Samples

Consistent with other studies (e.g., Karnik et al., 2009), we found that relative to non-offenders (35.4%), a higher proportion of young offenders (54.0%) have at least one EBP ($p < 0.0001$). That said, this prevalence rate among young offenders in the EPYC sample is substantially lower than other jurisdictions such as Malaysia (93.3%; Aida et al., 2014), South Korea (90.8%; Kim et al., 2017), Switzerland (82.6%; Heller et al., 2022), and the United States (between 60% and 90%; Fazel et al., 2008; Karnik et al., 2009; Teplin et al., 2002, 2012). While the prevalence for EBPs compares favourably with other jurisdictions, it is nonetheless important to address youths with problems, especially those with co-occurring conditions, as they are likely the ones with poorer prognosis and progress over time.

Approximately 1 in 2 (55% of offenders and 49% among non-offenders) of our young offenders and their non-offending counterparts with EBPs have co-occurring problems. That said, young offenders are not more likely ($p = 0.13$) to have co-occurring conditions relative to non-offenders. Our findings mirrored other epidemiological studies in showing high rates of comorbidity in different offending and non-offending samples (Angold et al., 1999; Kendler et al., 2003; Kessler et al., 2005; Kim et al., 2017).

There were differences in prevalence rates between young offenders and non-offenders in the types of EBPs. Overall, young offenders presented with higher prevalence of oppositional (20.2% offenders vs. 4.4% in non-offenders; $p < 0.0001$), and conduct problems (30.3% vs. 5.0%; $p < 0.0001$), as well as substance dependence (21.2% vs. 3.8%; $p < 0.0001$). Our findings mirror other reports that show an

Table 3.1 Percentage of male and female participants among young offenders and non-offenders that met the clinical criteria for EBPs (self-reported)

	Entire sample (n = 1,879)		Offenders (n = 1,224)		Non-offenders (n = 655)	
Problem	Females (%)	Males (%)	Females (%)	Males (%)	Females (%)	Males (%)
Depression	17.86	15.72	19.05	14.69	17.14	18.82
Anxiety problems	11.11	11.06	4.76	7.44	14.92	**22.06**
Somatic problems	3.97	4.88	2.12	3.87	5.08	7.94
ADHD	5.95	**9.16**	8.47	8.41	4.44	**11.47**
Oppositional problems	7.34	**17.38**	16.40	20.89	1.90	**6.76**
Conduct problems	11.51	**25.16**	26.46	30.95	2.54	**7.35**
Substance dependence	12.90	16.00	**26.98**	20.12	4.44	3.24

Note: Bold numbers denote statistically significant sex differences. Substance refers to alcohol and drug.

overrepresentation of these problems among young offenders (Beaudry et al., 2021; Rijo et al., 2016). These behavioural problems are posited to be early outward manifestations of delinquency (Jolliffe et al., 2019).

Young offenders are not more likely to have ADHD and depression relative to non-offenders ($ps > 0.13$). Unexpectedly, non-offenders had higher prevalence rates for anxiety (18.63% vs. 7.03%; $p < 0.0001$) and somatic problems relative to young offenders (6.56% vs. 3.59%; $p = 0.004$). One possible explanation for the higher prevalence of anxiety may be that the non-offender sample, all of whom were still schooling at the point of data collection, may be more anxious due to pressures of school. The lack of a significant difference in depression is also important in showing that depression is not likely to be a distinguishing factor between young offenders and non-offenders.

3.5.2 *Sex Differences*

Males (50.69%) were more likely than females (38.89%) to meet the clinical threshold for a self-reported EBP ($p < 0.0001$). Males were also more likely to have ADHD as well as oppositional and conduct problems (all $ps < 0.05$). See Table 3.1 for the breakdown by sample and sex.

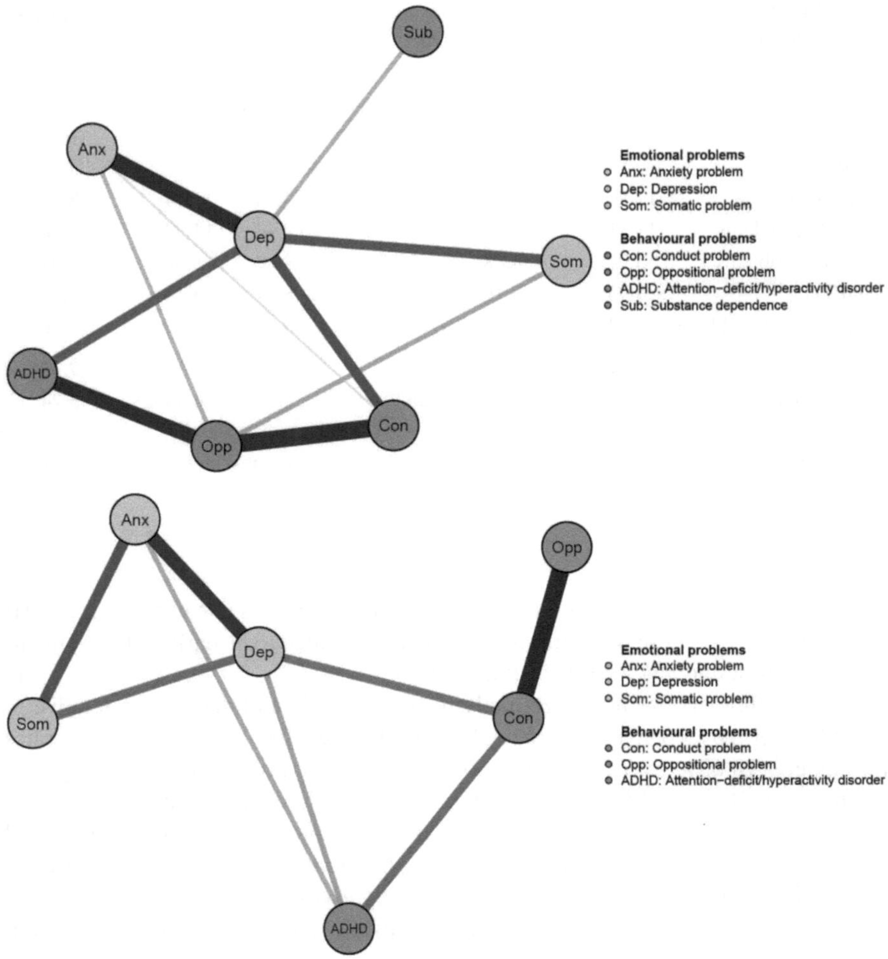

Fig. 3.1 Split networks of self-reported EBPs for young offenders (top) and non-offenders (bottom).
Note: The thickness of the edges represents the strength of the relationship between two nodes, controlling for all other variables in the network. For the non-offender network, substance dependence was dropped from the network as it did not have edges connecting to any nodes

3.6 Comparison of EBP Networks for Young Offenders and Non-offenders

The split networks for young offenders and non-offenders (see Fig. 3.1 top and Fig. 3.1 bottom) showed that *depression* was the most central node. The presence of depression was more likely to co-occur with other problems such as somatic and anxiety problems and with behavioural problems such as ADHD, and conduct problems. While we do not have the data on whether depression or other problems came first in our sample, a Danish national study showed that having mood disorders first poses significantly greater risk of developing other disorders as compared to those with other psychological problems as the index disorder (Plana-Ripoll et al., 2018). Our findings here, taken with others, therefore highlight the importance of treating depression early. Among young offenders, after depression, oppositional problem was the most central, as shown by its strong relationships with ADHD, and conduct problem (see also Appendix – Figs. 3.3 and 3.4 for young offenders, and non-offenders, respectively). Potentially, while the largest impact of intervention is on depression in this group, it is also worthwhile to address oppositional problem as this is likely to have strong reciprocal effects on ADHD, and conduct problems.

The strong connections between ADHD and oppositional as well as conduct problems in all our networks were unsurprising, considering the high degree of overlap between these problems' manifestations as mentioned previously (Harvey et al., 2016; Nock et al., 2007). This finding also concurred with others that pointed to shared genetic and environment factors (Burt et al., 2001; Eaves et al., 2000; Tuvblad et al., 2009). Likewise, the high probability of co-occurrence between anxiety problems and depression was predictable. It was reported that around 75% of people with anxiety disorders also met the clinical criteria for depression (Lamers et al., 2011).

3.7 Sex Specific Networks Among Young Offenders

For male and female young offenders, depression was again the most "central" node. In males, it had strong connections to anxiety, conduct, and somatic problems, as well as to ADHD. Oppositional problem likewise had strong connections to ADHD and conduct problem and relatively weaker connections to anxiety and somatic problems. In females, depression had strong connections with conduct and anxiety problems, as well as with ADHD. This pattern of findings suggests likewise that interventions for depression may result in large reciprocal effects on the other emotional and behavioural problems in the network (See Fig. 3.2).

3.8 Treatment Gap

We derived the treatment gap from the difference in the number of people who met the clinical threshold based on self-report, and the number of people who received a mental disorder diagnosis based on official records. This difference was then expressed as a percentage of those who met the clinical threshold based on self-report.

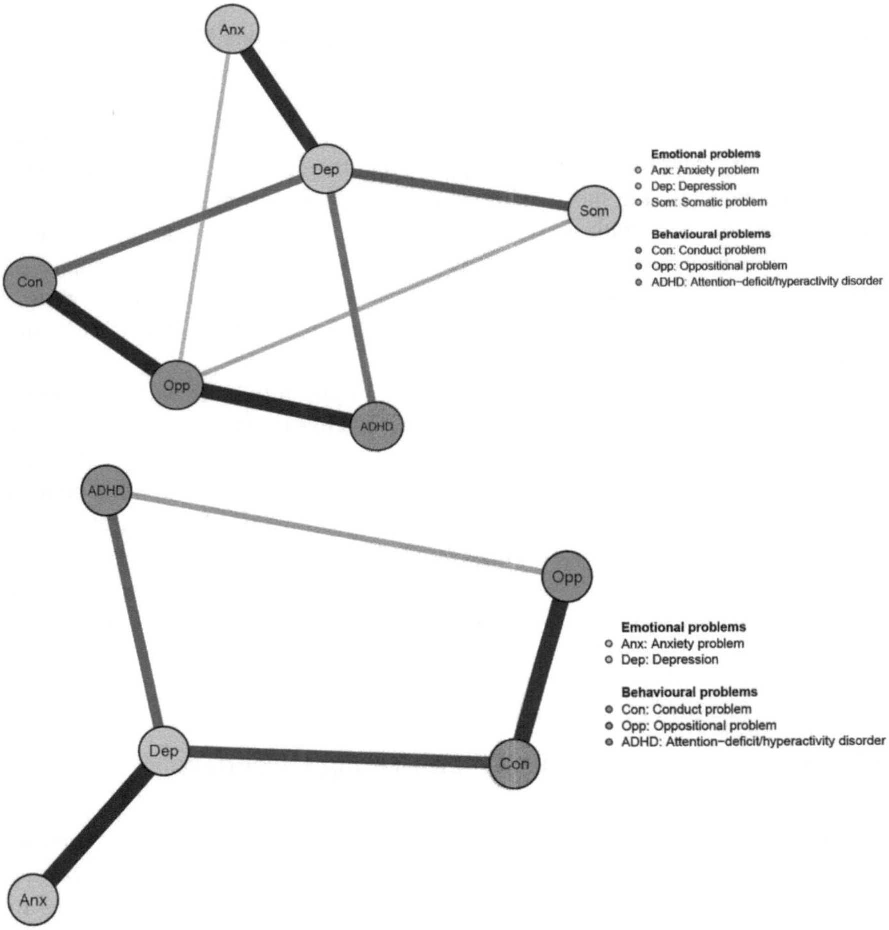

Fig. 3.2 Split network for male (top) and female (bottom) young offenders.
Note: The thickness of the edges represents the strength of the relationship between two nodes, controlling for all other variables in the network. For both male and female networks, substance dependence was removed, as the node did not have any edges connecting to any other node. For the female-specific network, somatic problem was removed due to its very low prevalence (*n* = 4)

Based on public healthcare records, we found that, out of 661 young offenders who had self-reported EBPs, 283 (42.81%) did not receive a diagnosis for a disorder from a public healthcare institution. Among the non-offenders, the percentage treatment gap is 65.9%, significantly larger than among the sample of young offenders ($p < 0.001$). The substantially smaller treatment gap in young offenders is promising, as it suggests that their emotional and behavioural problems were identified, which may in turn result in access to appropriate treatments. On the contrary, non-offending youths may largely go unnoticed within the school system, and may not get access to intervention early. Nevertheless, the treatment gap in both youth samples is substantially lower compared to the 78.6% reported in the Singapore Mental Health Study (Subramaniam et al., 2020). This may suggest improving mental health literacy among young persons. Follow-up studies on treatment gap among the Singapore population would validate this suggestion.

3.9 Practical Implications

Overall, the importance of depression in the comorbidity networks for young offenders and their non-offending counterparts suggests that it should be a priority to target it in any treatment plan. It has been shown that changes in highly influential nodes were more strongly associated with changes in the overall network, relative to other nodes (Robinaugh et al., 2016). Treating depression therefore should result in the largest reciprocal changes in other disorders in the network. While conduct and oppositional problems may be the most obvious to treat in offenders, as they are highly observable, and may impinge on risk/safety of self or others, our network indicated that depression should not be neglected. The call then is for practitioners to screen for emotional issues in intake interviews and at frequent intervals using psychometrically validated self-reports such as the Youth Self Report, the Beck Depression Inventory (BDI; Beck et al., 1996), or the Center for Epidemiologic Studies Depression Scale (CES-D; Radloff, 1977), so that depressive symptoms can be uncovered and intervened promptly.

Thorough and regular screenings for EBPs to complement administrative records take on even more significance considering the treatment gap experienced in our sample of young offenders, where it signifies that some have unmet mental health needs. This may be especially crucial for this group due to the elevated risk of re-offending (Guebert & Olver, 2014; McReynolds et al., 2010; Mulder et al., 2010). The relative lower treatment gap (42.81%) in young offenders in the current sample bodes well in that many of them have been identified in the healthcare system. That said, there is still a minority that have ongoing emotional or behavioural problems that are unidentified, suggesting a need for improved mental health literacy and screening in the schools and community.

While the focus of the current chapter was on young offenders, the relatively larger treatment gap in non-offenders means that careful attention needs to be paid as well to the well-being of non-offenders. These findings again call for efforts to increase mental health awareness among educators, parents and children, to be able to identify early warning signs of EBPs.

3.10 Future Directions

The findings in this chapter represent a first step in understanding the prevalence and comorbidity patterns among young offenders and non-offenders in Singapore through the EPYC study. While the prevalence rate among young offenders in our sample is substantially lower compared to other jurisdictions, continued vigilance in identifying those with EBPs is warranted. Currently, the empirical evidence is clear that untreated mental disorders multiply the risk of re-offending among these youths (Guebert & Olver, 2014; McReynolds et al., 2010; Mulder et al., 2010) and are associated with poorer outcomes later, such as adjustment problems, and substance use (Teplin et al., 2012; van der Molen et al., 2013). We suggest three potential areas of development to enhance the richness of future research. The first is to examine how different patterns of co-occurring disorders may amplify the risk of poorer rehabilitative outcomes. The second is whether these patterns vary according to different developmental taxonomies of offenders according to those proposed by Moffitt (1993). The third is to examine the developmental course of EBPs in young offenders, so that we can better understand whether the progression of these problems alter rehabilitative outcomes. In the subsequent chapter, we explore specifically the trajectory of depressive symptoms, given its importance as alluded to above. We believe that these endeavours will in turn allow for better profiling and understanding of young offenders and aid in rehabilitative efforts.

Appendix (Figs. 3.3 and 3.4)

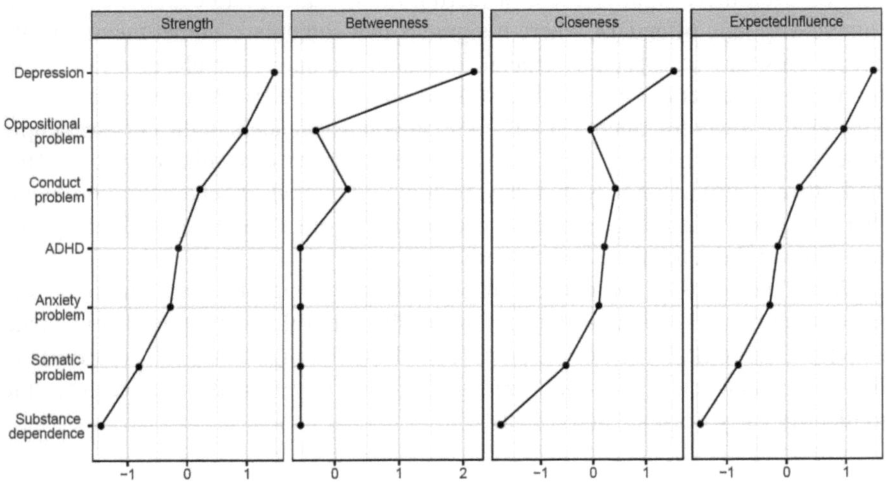

Fig. 3.3 Node strength centrality indices (z-transformed) for young offenders' network of EBPs

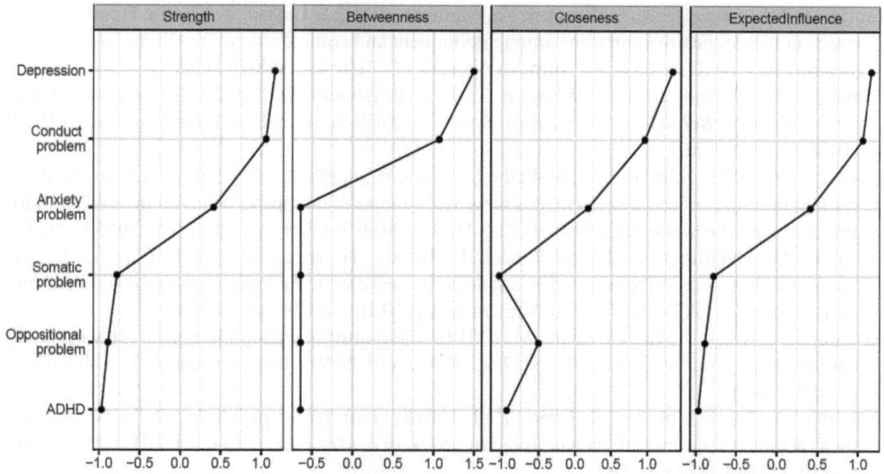

Fig. 3.4 Node strength centrality indices (z-transformed) for non-offenders' network of EBPs

References

Achenbach, T. M. (2001). *Manual for ASEBA school-age forms & profiles*. University of Vermont, Research Center for Children, Youth & Families.

Aida, S. A., Aili, H. H., Manveen, K. S., Salwina, W. I. W., Subash, K. P., Ng, C. G., & Muhsin, A. Z. M. (2014). Prevalence of psychiatric disorders among juvenile offenders in Malaysian prisons and association with socio-demographic and personal factors. *International Journal of Prisoner Health, 10*(2), 132–143. https://doi.org/10.1108/IJPH-06-2013-0029

Angold, A., Costello, E. J., & Erkanli, A. (1999). Comorbidity. *Journal of Child Psychology & Psychiatry, 40*(1), 57–87.

Beaudry, G., Yu, R., Långström, N., & Fazel, S. (2021). An updated systematic review and meta-regression analysis: Mental disorders among adolescents in juvenile detention and correctional facilities. *Journal of the American Academy of Child & Adolescent Psychiatry, 60*(1), 46–60. https://doi.org/10.1016/j.jaac.2020.01.015

Beck, A. T., Steer, R. A., & Brown, G. K. (1996). *Manual for the beck depression inventory-II*. Psychological Corporation.

Bhalla, I. P., Stefanovics, E. A., & Rosenheck, R. A. (2018). Mental health multimorbidity and poor quality of life in patients with schizophrenia. *Schizophrenia Research, 201*, 39–45. https://doi.org/10.1016/j.schres.2018.04.035

Borsboom, D., & Cramer, A. O. J. (2013). Network analysis: An integrative approach to the structure of psychopathology. *Annual Review of Clinical Psychology, 9*(1), 91–121. https://doi.org/10.1146/annurev-clinpsy-050212-185608

Boschloo, L., Schoevers, R. A., Borkulo, C. D. V., Borsboom, D., & Oldehinkel, A. J. (2016). The network structure of psychopathology in a community sample of preadolescents. *Journal of Abnormal Psychology, 125*(4), 599–606. https://doi.org/10.1037/abn0000150

Brown, T. A., Campbell, L. A., Lehman, C. L., Grisham, J. R., & Mancill, R. B. (2001). Current and lifetime comorbidity of the DSM-IV anxiety and mood disorders in a large clinical sample. *Journal of Abnormal Psychology, 110*(4), 585–599. https://doi.org/10.1037//0021-843x.110.4.585

Burt, S. A., Krueger, R. F., McGue, M., & Iacono, W. G. (2001). Sources of covariation among attention-deficit/hyperactivity disorder, oppositional defiant disorder, and conduct disorder: The importance of shared environment. *Journal of Abnormal Psychology, 110*(4), 516–525. https://doi.org/10.1037/0021-843x.110.4.516

Cauffman, E., Lexcen, F. J., Goldweber, A., Shulman, E. P., & Grisso, T. (2007). Gender differences in mental health symptoms among delinquent and community youth. *Youth Violence and Juvenile Justice, 5*(3), 287–307. https://doi.org/10.1177/1541204007301292

Cramer, A. O. J., Waldorp, L. J., Maas, H. L. J., & Borsboom, D. (2010). Comorbidity: A network analysis. *Behavioral and Brain Sciences, 33*(2–3), 137–150. https://doi.org/10.1017/s0140525x09991567

Eaves, L., Rutter, M., Silberg, J. L., Shillady, L., Maes, H., & Pickles, A. (2000). Genetic and environmental causes of covariation in interview assessments of disruptive behavior in child and adolescent twins. *Behavior Genetics, 30*(4), 321–334. https://doi.org/10.1023/A:1026553518272

Elovainio, M., Hakulinen, C., Pulkki-Råback, L., Raaska, H., & Lapinleimu, H. (2018). The network structure of childhood psychopathology in international adoptees. *Journal of Child and Family Studies, 27*(7), 2161–2170. https://doi.org/10.1007/s10826-018-1046-z

Epskamp, S., Kruis, J., & Marsman, M. (2017). Estimating psychopathological networks: Be careful what you wish for. *PLoS One, 12*(6), e0179891. https://doi.org/10.1371/journal.pone.0179891

Epskamp, S., Borsboom, D., & Fried, E. I. (2018). Estimating psychological networks and their accuracy: A tutorial paper. *Behavior Research Methods, 50*(1), 195–212. https://doi.org/10.3758/s13428-017-0862-1

Fazel, S., Doll, H., & Långström, N. (2008). Mental disorders among adolescents in juvenile detention and correctional facilities: A systematic review and metaregression analysis of 25 surveys. *Journal of the American Academy of Child and Adolescent Psychiatry, 47*(9), 1010–1019. https://doi.org/10.1097/CHI.ObO13e31817eecf3

Guebert, A. F., & Olver, M. E. (2014). An examination of criminogenic needs, mental health concerns, and recidivism in a sample of violent young offenders: Implications for risk, need, and responsivity. *International Journal of Forensic Mental Health, 13*(4), 295–310. https://doi.org/10.1080/14999013.2014.955220

Hartsell, E. N. (2021). The relationship between psychological symptom ratings and crime in juvenile justice system involved young people. *Criminal Behaviour and Mental Health, 31*(1), 13–30. https://doi.org/10.1002/cbm.2169

Harvey, E. A., Breaux, R. P., & Lugo-Candelas, C. I. (2016). Early development of comorbidity between symptoms of attention-deficit/hyperactivity disorder (ADHD) and oppositional defiant disorder (ODD). *Journal of Abnormal Psychology, 125*(2), 154–167. https://doi.org/10.1037/abn0000090

Heller, P., Morosan, L., Badoud, D., Laubscher, M., Olariaga, L. J., Debbane, M., Wolff, H., & Baggio, S. (2022). Prevalence rates and evolution of psychiatric disorders among incarcerated youths in comparison with non-incarcerated youths. *Frontiers in Psychiatry, 12*, 784954. https://doi.org/10.3389/fpsyt.2021.784954

Hevey, D. (2018). Network analysis: A brief overview and tutorial. *Health Psychology and Behavioral Medicine, 6*(1), 301–328. https://doi.org/10.1080/21642850.2018.1521283

Ishikawa, H., Kawakami, N., & Kessler, R. C. (2016). Lifetime and 12-month prevalence, severity and unmet need for treatment of common mental disorders in Japan: Results from the final dataset of world mental health Japan survey. *Epidemiology and Psychiatric Sciences, 25*(3), 217–229. https://doi.org/10.1017/S2045796015000566

Jolliffe, D., Farrington, D. P., Brunton-Smith, I., Loeber, R., Ahonen, L., & Palacios, A. P. (2019). Depression, anxiety and delinquency: Results from the Pittsburgh youth study. *Journal of Criminal Justice, 62*, 42–49. https://doi.org/10.1016/j.jcrimjus.2018.08.004

Karnik, N. S., Soller, M., Redlich, A., Silverman, M., Kraemer, H. C., Haapanen, R., & Steiner, H. (2009). Prevalence of and gender differences in psychiatric disorders among juvenile delinquents incarcerated for nine months. *Psychiatric Services, 60*(6), 838–841. https://doi.org/10.1176/ps.2009.60.6.838

Kaufmann, T., Alnæs, D., Doan, N. T., Brandt, C. L., Andreassen, O. A., & Westlye, L. T. (2017). Delayed stabilization and individualization in connectome development are related to psychiatric disorders. *Nature Neuroscience, 20*(4), 513–515. https://doi.org/10.1038/nn.4511

Kendler, K. S., Prescott, C. A., Myers, J., & Neale, M. C. (2003). The structure of genetic and environmental risk factors for common psychiatric and substance use disorders in men and women. *Archives of General Psychiatry, 60*(9), 929–937. https://doi.org/10.1001/archpsyc.60.9.929

Kessler, R. C., Berglund, P., Demler, O., Jin, R., Merikangas, K. R., & Walters, E. E. (2005). Lifetime prevalence and age-of-onset distributions of DSM-IV disorders in the national comorbidity survey replication. *Archives of General Psychiatry, 62*(6), 593–602. https://doi.org/10.1001/archpsyc.62.6.593

Kessler, R. C., Avenevoli, S., McLaughlin, K. A., Green, J. G., Lakoma, M. D., Petukhova, M., Pine, D. S., Sampson, N. A., Zaslavsky, A. M., & Merikangas, K. R. (2012). Lifetime co-morbidity of DSM-IV disorders in the US National comorbidity survey replication adolescent supplement (NCS-A). *Psychological Medicine, 42*(9), 1997–2010. https://doi.org/10.1017/S0033291712000025

Kim, J. I., Kim, B., Kim, B.-N., Hong, S.-B., Lee, D. W., Chung, J.-Y., Choi, J. Y., Choi, B.-S., Oh, Y.-R., & Youn, M. (2017). Prevalence of psychiatric disorders, comorbidity patterns, and repeat offending among male juvenile detainees in South Korea: A cross-sectional study. *Child and Adolescent Psychiatry and Mental Health, 11*(1), 6. https://doi.org/10.1186/s13034-017-0143-x

Kohn, R., Saxena, S., Levav, I., & Saraceno, B. (2004). The treatment gap in mental health care. *Bulletin of the World Health Organization, 82*(11), 858–866.

Kohn, R., Ali, A. A., Puac-Polanco, V., Figueroa, C., López-Soto, V., Morgan, K., Saldivia, S., & Vicente, B. (2018). Mental health in the Americas: An overview of the treatment gap. *Revista Panamericana de Salud Publica Pan American Journal of Public Health, 42*, 165. https://doi.org/10.26633/RPSP.2018.165

Lamers, F., van Oppen, P., Comijs, H. C., Smit, J. H., Spinhoven, P., van Balkom, A. J., Nolen, W. A., Zitman, F. G., Beekman, A. T., & Penninx, B. W. (2011). Comorbidity patterns of anxiety and depressive disorders in a large cohort study: The Netherlands study of depression and anxiety (NESDA). *The Journal of Clinical Psychiatry, 72*(3), 341–348. https://doi.org/10.4088/JCP.10m06176blu

Livanou, M., Furtado, V., & Singh, S. (2016). Prevalence and nature of mental disorders among young offenders in custody and community: A meta-analysis. *European Psychiatry, 33*, S460. https://doi.org/10.1016/j.eurpsy.2016.01.1675

Loeber, R., & Farrington, D. P. (2000). Young children who commit crime: Epidemiology, developmental origins, risk factors, early interventions, and policy implications. *Development and Psychopathology, 12*(4), 737–762. https://doi.org/10.1017/S0954579400004107

McCuish, E., Bouchard, M., Beauregard, E., & Corrado, R. (2019). A network approach to understanding the structure of core symptoms of psychopathic personality disturbance in adolescent offenders. *Journal of Abnormal Child Psychology, 47*(9), 1467–1482. https://doi.org/10.1007/s10802-019-00530-9

McNally, R. J. (2020). Network analysis of psychopathology: Controversies and challenges. *Annual Review of Clinical Psychology, 17*, 31–53. https://doi.org/10.1146/annurev-clinpsy-081219-092850

McReynolds, L. S., Schwalbe, C. S., & Wasserman, G. A. (2010). The contribution of psychiatric disorder to juvenile recidivism. *Criminal Justice and Behavior, 37*(2), 204–216. https://doi.org/10.1177/0093854809354961

Michel, C., Schnyder, N., Schmidt, S. J., Groth, N., Schimmelmann, B. G., & Schultze-Lutter, F. (2018). Functioning mediates help-seeking for mental problems in the general population. *European Psychiatry, 54*, 1–9. https://doi.org/10.1016/j.eurpsy.2018.06.009

Moffitt, T. E. (1993). Adolescence-limited and life-course-persistent antisocial behavior: A developmental taxonomy. *Psychological Review, 100*, 674–701.

Mulder, E., Brand, E., Bullens, R., & Van Marle, H. (2010). A classification of risk factors in serious juvenile offenders and the relation between patterns of risk factors and recidivism. *Criminal Behavior and Mental Health, 20*(1), 23–38. https://doi.org/10.1002/cbm.754

Nock, M. K., Kazdin, A. E., Hiripi, E., & Kessler, R. C. (2007). Lifetime prevalence, correlates, and persistence of oppositional defiant disorder: Results from the National Comorbidity Survey Replication. *The Journal of Child Psychology and Psychiatry, 48*(7), 703–713. https://doi.org/10.1111/j.1469-7610.2007.01733.x

Ottosen, C., Petersen, L., Larsen, J. T., & Dalsgaard, S. (2016). Gender differences in associations between attention-deficit/hyperactivity disorder and substance use disorder. *Journal of the American Academy of Child & Adolescent Psychiatry, 55*(3), 227–234. https://doi.org/10.1016/j.jaac.2015.12.010

Plana-Ripoll, O., Pedersen, C. B., Holtz, Y., Benros, M. E., Dalsgaard, S., de Jonge, P., Fan, C. C., Degenhardt, L., Ganna, A., Greve, A. N., Gunn, J., Iburg, K. M., Kessing, L. V., Lee, B. K., Lim, C. C. W., Mors, O., Nordentoft, M., Prior, A., Roest, A. M., et al. (2018). Exploring comorbidity within mental disorders among a Danish national population. *JAMA Psychiatry, 76*(3), 259–270. https://doi.org/10.1001/jamapsychiatry.2018.3658

Pokorny, A. D., Miller, B. A., & Kaplan, H. B. (1972). The brief MAST: A shortened version of the Michigan alcoholism screening test. *American Journal of Psychiatry, 129*, 342–345. https://doi.org/10.1176/ajp.129.3.342

Radloff, L. S. (1977). The CES-D scale: A self-report depression scale for research in the general population. *Applied Psychological Measurement, 1*(3), 385–401. https://doi.org/10.1177/014662167700100306

Rijo, D., Brazão, N., Barroso, R., Silva, D. R., Vagos, P., Vieira, A., Lavado, A., & Macedo, A. M. (2016). Mental health problems in male young offenders in custodial versus community based-programs: Implications for juvenile justice interventions. *Child and Adolescent Psychiatry and Mental Health, 10*(1), 40. https://doi.org/10.1186/s13034-016-0131-6

Robinaugh, D. J., Millner, A. J., & McNally, R. J. (2016). Identifying highly influential nodes in the complicated grief network. *Journal of Abnormal Psychology, 125*(6), 747–757. https://doi.org/10.1037/abn0000181

Seena, F., Helen, D., & Niklas, L. (2008). Mental disorders among adolescents in juvenile detention and correctional facilities: A systematic review and metaregression analysis of 25 surveys. *Journal of the American Academy of Child & Adolescent Psychiatry, 47*(9), 1010–1019. https://doi.org/10.1097/CHI.0b013e31817eecf3

Sherbourne, C. D., & Wells, K. B. (1997). Course of depression in patients with comorbid anxiety disorders. *Journal of Affective Disorders, 43*(3), 245–250. https://doi.org/10.1016/S0165-0327(97)01442-0

Skinner, H. A. (1982). The drug abuse screening test. *Addictive Behaviors, 7*(4), 363–371. https://doi.org/10.1016/0306-4603(82)90005-3

Stewart, S. L., Thornley, E., Lapshina, N., Erickson, P., Vingilis, E., Hamilton, H., & Kolla, N. (2020). Sex differences in youth with mental health problems in inpatient, outpatient and youth justice settings. *BMC Psychiatry, 20*(1), 11. https://doi.org/10.1186/s12888-019-2413-z

Subramaniam, M., Abdin, E., Vaingankar, J. A., Shafie, S., Chua, H. C., Tan, W. M., Tan, K. B., Verma, S., Heng, D., & Chong, S. A. (2020). Minding the treatment gap: Results of the Singapore mental health study. *Social Psychiatry and Psychiatric Epidemiology, 55*(11), 1415–1424. https://doi.org/10.1007/s00127-019-01748-0

Teplin, L. A., Abram, K. M., McClelland, G. M., Dulcan, M. K., & Mericle, A. A. (2002). Psychiatric disorders in youth in juvenile detention. *Archives of General Psychiatry, 59*(12), 1133–1143. https://doi.org/10.1001/archpsyc.59.12.1133

Teplin, L. A., Welty, L. J., Abram, K. M., Dulcan, M. K., & Washburn, J. J. (2012). Prevalence and persistence of psychiatric disorders in youth after detention: A prospective longitudinal study. *Archives of General Psychiatry, 69*(10), 1031–1043. https://doi.org/10.1001/archgenpsychiatry.2011.2062

Tuvblad, C., Zheng, M., Raine, A., & Baker, L. A. (2009). A common genetic factor explains the covariation among ADHD, ODD and CD symptoms in 9-10 year old boys and girls. *Journal of Abnormal Child Psychology, 37*(2), 153–167. https://doi.org/10.1007/s10802-008-9278-9

Underwood, L. A., & Washington, A. (2016). Mental illness and juvenile offenders. *International Journal of Environmental Research and Public Health, 13*(2), 228. https://doi.org/10.3390/ijerph13020228

van den Berg, J. W., Smid, W., Kossakowski, J. J., van Beek, D., Borsboom, D., Janssen, E., & Gijs, L. (2020). The application of network analysis to dynamic risk factors in adult male sex offenders. *Clinical Psychological Science, 8*(3), 539–554. https://doi.org/10.1177/2167702620901720

van der Molen, E., Vermeiren, R. R., Krabbendam, A. A., Beekman, A. T., Doreleijers, T. A., & Jansen, L. M. (2013). Detained adolescent females' multiple mental health and adjustment problem outcomes in young adulthood. *The Journal of Child Psychology and Psychiatry, 54*(9), 950–957. https://doi.org/10.1111/jcpp.12044

Wasserman, G. A., McReynolds, L. S., Ko, S. J., Katz, L. M., & Carpenter, J. R. (2005). Gender differences in psychiatric disorders at juvenile probation intake. *American Journal of Public Health, 95*(1), 131–137. https://doi.org/10.2105/AJPH.2003.024737

Weissman, M. M., Wolk, S., Wickramaratne, P., Goldstein, R. B., Adams, P., Greenwald, S., Ryan, N. D., Dahl, R. E., & Steinberg, D. (1999). Children with prepubertal-onset major depressive disorder and anxiety grown up. *Archives of General Psychiatry, 56*(9), 794–801. https://doi.org/10.1001/archpsyc.56.9.794

Zhou, Y., Cao, Z., Yang, M., Xi, X., Guo, Y., Fang, M., Cheng, L., & Du, Y. (2017). Comorbid generalized anxiety disorder and its association with quality of life in patients with major depressive disorder. *Scientific Reports, 7*(1), 40511. https://doi.org/10.1038/srep4051

Chapter 4
Prevalence and Trajectories of Depression

Dongdong Li

Contents

Depression is one of the leading causes of illness and disability for adolescents and is among the top contributors to disease burden (World Health Organization, 2021). The annual societal costs, which refer to the total burden imposed on the society each year, are 99 times as high for families with a clinically depressed adolescent compared to the general population (Bodden et al., 2018). In addition, youth involved in the juvenile justice system were found to have much higher levels of depression throughout adolescence and early adulthood (Gaete et al., 2018), with depression, suicide and violent behaviours often co-occurring (Ozkan et al., 2019). Elevated levels of depression were found to increase reintegration barriers (Semenza & Link, 2019), and depression as a mental health indicator was recommended to be used as an alternative measure of success/failure after release (National Academies of Sciences, Engineering, & Medicine, 2022). Therefore, identifying the prevalence

D. Li (✉)
Translational Social Research Division, National Council of Social Service, Singapore, Singapore
e-mail: li_dongdong@ncss.gov.sg

D. Li et al. (eds.), *Emotional and Behavioural Problems of Young Offenders in Singapore*, SpringerBriefs in Criminology,
https://doi.org/10.1007/978-3-031-41702-3_4

and trajectories of depression, as well as the risk and protective factors for depression, is imperative for the rehabilitation of young offenders.

This chapter focuses on two depression-related outcomes: *Depression* as a binary variable and *Depression Severity* as a continuous variable. The main aim of the chapter is to investigate the percentage of young offenders with *Depression* around the time when they committed a crime and how this condition changed in the subsequent 2 years. In addition, this chapter studies the risk and protective factors of *Depression Severity*. The purpose is to find out what the important predictors of *Depression Severity* are when these youths first enter the justice system, as well as what factors contribute to the change in *Depression Severity* over time.

4.1 Prevalence of Depression

Depression is a common mood disorder, with emotional, behavioural, cognitive, social, and biological symptoms that cause the subject to malfunction in his/her environment (Bernard, 2018). Studies in different countries or jurisdictions using different measures reported varying prevalence rates of depression among young offenders. Based on a study of 1,024 incarcerated adolescents in the USA, 47% had moderate to severe depression, and 10% had major depressive disorder with no gender differences. Of the depressed youths, only 20% had been previously diagnosed and treated (Domalanta et al., 2003). In Brazil, 28% of young offenders were found to have moderate to severe depression (da Silva et al., 2021). In Asia, depression is also examined in young offenders. Among 1505 incarcerated youths in Taiwan, the prevalence of depression was shown to be 34.7% (Lyu et al., 2015). In China, more than half of the 323 incarcerated male youths had higher than criterion scores for depression (Zhou et al., 2014). Similar to the China study, 48.1% were classified as "being depressed" in a group of Japanese female young offenders with serious offenses (Matsuura et al., 2013). Despite the differences in these prevalence rates, one consistent finding is that depression is highly prevalent among young offenders.

Time might also be an important factor that contributed to the differences in prevalence between studies. Among the general population in the USA, there is a steady increase in mood disorder over time, with rates of major depressive episodes increasing from 8.7% in 2005 to 13.2% in 2017 among adolescents (Twenge et al., 2019). Using a large sample of 11,669 young offenders in the USA, the prevalence of major depressive episodes among females increased from 24.4% to 33.0% between 2005 and 2014, but no significant trend changes were observed among males (Holzer et al., 2018). A recent meta-analysis synthesising the literature on adolescents in juvenile detention and correctional facilities revealed that the prevalence of major depression was 10.1% among males and 25.8% among females; the prevalence rate was found to be slightly lower for studies published after 2006 although the effect did not reach statistical significance at $p = 0.05$ (Beaudry et al., 2021).

In our study, DSM-oriented depression was examined using 13 statements from the Youth Self-Report and Adult Self-Report, which screen youth and adults for emotional and behavioural problems (Achenbach, 2001). These statements include "I feel worthless or inferior" and "I am unhappy, sad or depressed". The youth rated each statement on a three-point scale from "Not True" to "Very True or Often True". The ratings were summed and converted into a *T*-score, which was used to represent *Depression Severity*. Youth with a *T*-score of 70 or higher were categorised as having scores in the clinical range and thus deemed to have *Depression*. As presented in Chap. 3, the prevalence of *Depression* at the start of the study using all three cohorts was 14.69% among male young offenders and 19.05% among females.

4.2 Changes in Depression

Despite many studies indicating a high prevalence of depression among young offenders, few studies have tracked changes in depression over time after youths enter the justice system. Among 283 high-risk youths from the Chicago Youth Development Study, emotional problems (such as depression) showed a linear decreasing trend over 4 years for most of the offenders (Sheidow et al., 2008). The only exception was for those who escalated to more serious antisocial behaviours; this group did not experience the typical decrease in emotional problems. Instead, they had an essentially flat trajectory. In a Swiss study of 86 incarcerated youths, their short stay in a detention centre (median: 41.5 days of stay) was associated with a desirable change in behavioural but not in emotional problems (Heller et al., 2022). In another study of 1,216 male young offenders, using longer follow-ups in 3 demographically distinct regions in the USA, it was found that depressive symptoms declined initially after arrest, followed by an upward turn occurring a few years later (Baker et al., 2022). These findings seemed to suggest that emotional problems are stable in the short term after these youths enter the justice system, decrease within 1 or 2 years' time and increase again after that. However, these studies only examined changes in depression as a continuous variable (i.e., the severity of depression). None of the studies explored changes in depression as a binary variable. In other words, few studies followed the same sample and examined the change in depression prevalence over time.

In this study, we examined the change in the prevalence of *Depression* over 3 waves among a subgroup of 543 young offenders from the first 2 cohorts who completed all 3 waves. This subgroup did not differ from the overall sample in terms of age, race, and sex, with a mean age of 17.5 years ($SD = 1.5$), and 85% were males. Almost four-fifths (79%) of this subsample were placed under the supervision of the Ministry of Social and Family Development, similar to 76% of the overall sample.

Across the three time points, the observed proportion of *Depression* in young offenders decreased (15%, 10%, and 6% respectively). Latent growth curve models (LGCM) with random intercept and linear random slopes fitted the data well, indicating that the decrease was a linear trend. To further check the potential effects from missing data, the analysis was repeated on the overall sample from the first two cohorts as a comparison. The overall prevalence rates were the same for the three waves (Table 4.1).

The prevalence of *Depression* is also disaggregated based on age and sex as shown in Table 4.1. Sex differences at each wave were not significant, although a higher proportion of females had *Depression* compared to males at all three time points. For females, the prevalence dropped from 21% to 7%, while for males, it dropped from 14% to 6%. Separate LGCM models on both sexes showed a linear decrease with a good model data fit. Similarly, the age differences at all three time points were nonsignificant. The proportion of *Depression* in young offenders decreased in all age groups from Wave 1 to Wave 3.

To further examine whether these youths with *Depression* at baseline stayed in the clinical range across time, the findings are represented in scattered boxplots as shown in Fig. 4.1. Red dots represented those youths with *Depression*, while the grey dots were those below a *T*-score of 70. A number was used to represent each of these youths who had *Depression* for all three waves. It is obvious that majority of the young offenders did not stay equally depressed over all three waves. Take youth aged 12 to 16 for example: only one of the males and none of the females stayed in the clinical range over time. Out of the 82 females, only 3 (3.7%) stayed in the clinical range over all 3 waves. All these three females were older than 18 years at the start of the study. Out of the 461 males, 9 (2%) of them stayed in the clinical range and 8 of these chronic cases were aged 17 years and above at the start.

To provide a more comprehensive perspective, we also compared the subgroups using the distribution of *Depression Severity* as presented in Fig. 4.1, charted based on age, sex, and wave. As shown in the figure, the average scores for *Depression Severity* were also on a decreasing trend over time for most of the subgroups, consistent with the analysis on *Depression* as a binary variable. This decreasing trend in *Depression Severity* was also formally tested using LGCM. The average baseline *Depression Severity* was 60.94, and there was significant variability in these scores across individuals at baseline ($p < 0.001$). On average, *Depression Severity* decreased by 2.30 points each year, with a significant variance of 8.69 points, suggesting that the severity did not decrease at the same rate for all participants. In fact, some had increased levels of depressive symptomatology as evidenced by the higher scores on the scale. The baseline score and the change in *Depression Severity* were negatively associated, indicating that those with higher depression levels at the beginning of the study were more likely to experience a sharper decline over time.

4.3 Risk and Protective Factors Relating to Depression

Numerous studies on the predictors of depression identified adverse childhood experiences (ACE) as strong risk factors (Baek et al., 2019). For example, higher scores on child maltreatment (Burlaka et al., 2020; Gaete et al., 2018) and multiple types of maltreatment (Clements-Nolle & Waddington, 2019; Pengpid & Peltzer,

Table 4.1 Prevalence of depression by age, sex, wave, and participation status

	Participation status			Sex			Age at baseline			
Depression	All three waves ($n = 543$)	All available data ($n = 835$)	p^a	Male ($n = 461$)	Female ($n = 82$)	p	12–16 ($n = 92$)	17–18 ($n = 220$)	18–19 ($n = 231$)	p
W1	82 (15%)	115 (15%)	0.81	65 (14%)	17 (21%)	0.30	16 (17%)	31 (14%)	35 (15%)	0.91
W2	57 (10%)	79 (10%)	1.00	46 (10%)	11 (13%)	0.65	11 (12%)	28 (13%)	18 (8%)	0.37
W3	34 (6%)	37 (6%)	0.98	28 (6%)	6 (7%)	0.91	7 (8%)	15 (7%)	12 (5%)	0.84

[a]This p value is based on the comparison between those who participated in all three waves and those who only participated in one or two waves

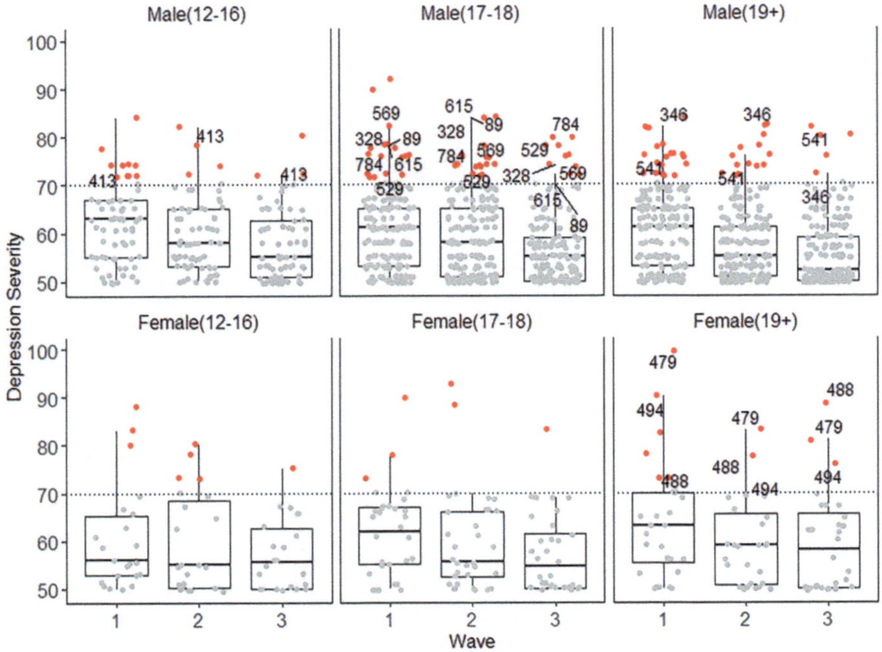

Fig. 4.1 Depression by age, sex, and wave

2020; Wanklyn et al., 2012) were associated with more severe depressive symptoms, with emotional abuse as one of the strongest predictors of depressive affect (Jencks & Leibowitz, 2018) and suicidal ideation (Kenny et al., 2008). Among incarcerated youth, childhood maltreatment and sexual abuse were shown to be significant risk factors for depression as well (Gover, 2004; Gover & MacKenzie, 2003).

Besides child maltreatment, other types of early violence exposure were also identified as significant risk factors for depression. For example, early exposure to family violence was found to have both direct and indirect effects on later depressive symptoms through physical punishment and bullying victimisation (Huang et al., 2021). Youth who experienced stable high exposure to community violence consistently suffered worse mental health problems, such as depression and anxiety (Baskin & Sommers, 2015). Peer victimisation was also found to be strongly related to suicidal thoughts and attempts (Hinduja & Patchin, 2010; van Geel et al., 2014).

Personality traits that could make an individual vulnerable to affective problems (Kotov et al., 2010) and physical health issues that hinder daily functioning are also significant risk factors for depression (Alves Donato et al., 2021; Lyu et al., 2015). Studies have suggested that physical fitness is particularly protective for adolescents who are high in neuroticism (Yeatts et al., 2017). In terms of other protective factors, strong personal resilience (e.g., high coping skills, as well as strong social networks and resilient role models) was shown to be helpful in alleviating depressive symptomatology (Southwick & Charney, 2012).

In the present study, risk and protective factors for *Depression Severity* were examined using the overall sample including a total of 835 young offenders from the first 2 cohorts. The numbers of these youths who participated in the interviews for the three waves were 790, 755, and 598 respectively. No missing values were found for the demographic variables, and the missing pattern is *Missing At Random*. Robust maximum likelihood (MLR) was used to deal with missing data in these models, providing correct estimates with robust standard errors (Larsen, 2011).

Depression Severity was used as the main outcome variable. *Depression* as a binary variable was not used in this analysis because of the small number of these youths having *Depression* at Wave 3. A list of predictors measured at baseline was used in the analysis to determine the between-individual effects. These variables include the demographic data (*Age*, *Race*, *Sex*, *Placement*, *Socio-economic Status* as measured by whether the participant lived in a rental flat under the Public Rental Scheme), risk factors (*Physical* and *Mental Health Visits* as measured by the number of visits to health institutions due to physical or mental health conditions, *Neuroticism* measured by 12 items from the NEO-FFI-3, 12 types of *ACEs* in the first 18 years of their lives), and protective factors measured as *Assets* from internal, school, work, home, peer, and community domains. A detailed description of the risk and protective factors can be found in Chap. 2.

Because of the large number of predictors, they were first entered into the model one by one in a series of bivariate analyses. The predictors which were not significantly associated with both the intercept and the slope of the outcome variables at $p = 0.05$ were then removed from further analysis. As a result, *Age*, *Race*, *Physical Health Visits*, *Household Member Incarceration*, *Parental Separation*, *Internal Assets*, *Community Assets*, and *Workplace Assets* were removed. These variables were not associated with both the baseline score and the change in *Depression Severity*.

After removing the nonsignificant variables from the bivariate analysis, all the remaining predictors were entered into one model (see Table 4.2). The factors that were significantly associated with higher baseline *Depression Severity* included *Neuroticism* and all types of early violence exposure. These multiple types of violence exposure consisted of *Community Violence*, *Peer Victimisation*, *Family Violence*, *Emotional/Physical Abuse*, and *Sexual Abuse*. Each of these factors made a unique contribution to the baseline *Depression Severity* score. While controlling for these factors, other household disadvantages like *Living in Public Rental Housing* and *Household Mental Illness* were not significantly associated with *Depression Severity* anymore.

Although a number of the predictors were significantly associated with *Depression Severity* at baseline as shown above, not all had significant effects on the change in *Depression Severity* over time. For example, among young offenders, those with *Physical/Emotional Abuse* had higher levels of *Depression Severity* across all three waves, so the change pattern did not differ significantly between those with or without such abuse (Fig. 4.2a). However, two exceptions were found

Table 4.2 Regression coefficients of the LGCM model on depression severity

	Intercept		*Slope*	
	Estimate (standard errors)	*p*	Estimate (standard errors)	*p*
Female	−0.63(0.71)	0.374	0.44(0.47)	0.339
Order supervised by MSF	−0.59(0.55)	0.284	0.75(0.40)[#]	0.059
Public rental	0.01(0.55)	0.982	0.90(0.43)[*]	0.037
Neuroticism	7.57(0.50)[***]	0.001	−2.51(0.33)[***]	0.001
Mental health visits	0.96(0.54)[#]	0.075	−0.20(0.29)	0.492
Community violence	1.73(0.63)[**]	0.006	−0.82(0.39)[*]	0.033
Peer victimisation	1.82(0.90)[*]	0.043	−0.80(0.58)	0.167
Household substance abuse	−0.21(0.56)	0.713	0.71(0.39)#	0.072
Household mental illness	0.12(0.79)	0.884	0.63(0.56)	0.259
Home violence	1.14(0.55)[*]	0.039	−0.44(0.37)	0.242
Emotional/physical abuse	1.60(0.69)[*]	0.020	−0.13(0.43)	0.762
Sexual abuse	1.92(0.77)[*]	0.012	0.26(0.54)	0.632
Emotional neglect	0.60(0.52)	0.244	0.11(0.34)	0.756
Physical neglect	0.58(0.86)	0.496	−0.48(0.60)	0.423
Home assets	−0.42(0.45)	0.353	−0.66(0.29)[*]	0.020
School assets	0.38(0.27)	0.152	−0.25(0.18)	0.171
Peer assets	−0.53(0.47)	0.261	−0.09(0.32)	0.783

Note: *LGCM* latent growth curve model
$\#p < 0.1$ $*p < 0.05$ $**p < 0.01$ $***p < 0.001$

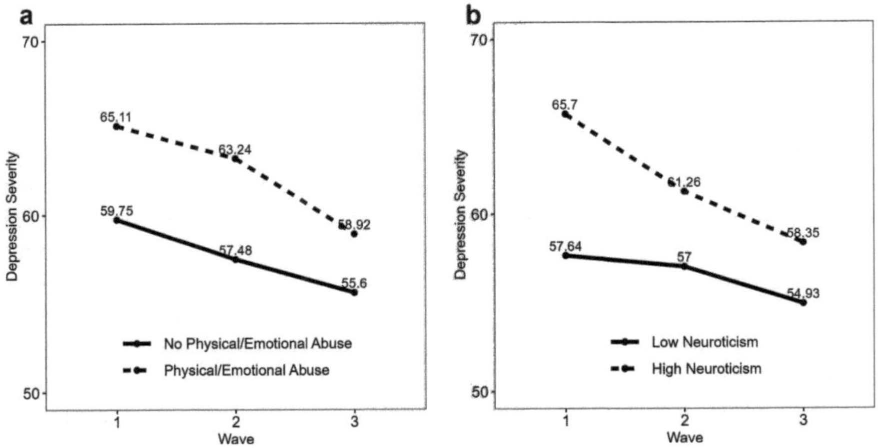

Fig. 4.2 Change in depression severity by physical/emotional abuse and neuroticism

for young offenders. For those with high *Neuroticism* and *Community Violence* at the start; *Depression Severity* decreased more sharply with time (Fig. 4.2b). This decrease was made more apparent while comparing to those with low *Neuroticism* or low *Community Violence*, who did not have very high levels of *Depression Severity* at baseline to start with, resulting in a relatively small decrease in comparison.

Controlling for the other covariates, another significant risk factor for change in *Depression Severity* was *Living in Public Rental Housing*. Among young offenders, those from these disadvantaged low-income households showed lesser improvement in *Depression Severity* compared to others. As shown in Fig. 4.3a, the decrease in *Depression Severity* was smaller over time among those who lived in public rental housing, resulting in a larger gap between the two groups at Wave 3.

For protective factors, *Assets from the Home Environment* was the most significant factor associated with depression trajectories. The general trend in young offenders is that those with higher levels of *Home Assets* at baseline had more improvement in *Depression Severity* over time. For illustrative purposes, the continuous *Home Asset* variable was divided into low [0–2], moderate (2–3], and high *Home Assets* (3–4]. From Fig. 4.3b, the difference in the change of *Depression Severity* is mainly from those with low Home Assets, whose level of *Depression Severity* did not follow the general decreasing trend. Their *Depression Severity* did not change for the better over time. Young offenders with either moderate or high *Home Assets* had decreased *Depression Severity* in similar patterns.

Multigroup analysis was also conducted on *Depression Severity*, with grouping by the demographic variables. Models with equal regression constraints all achieved good model fit for *Sex*, *Race*, *Age*, and *Place of Order*. Likelihood ratio tests for model comparisons were nonsignificant, which suggested that equal regression was supported for these variables. In other words, the predictors as shown in Table 4.2 were similar for different demographic subgroups.

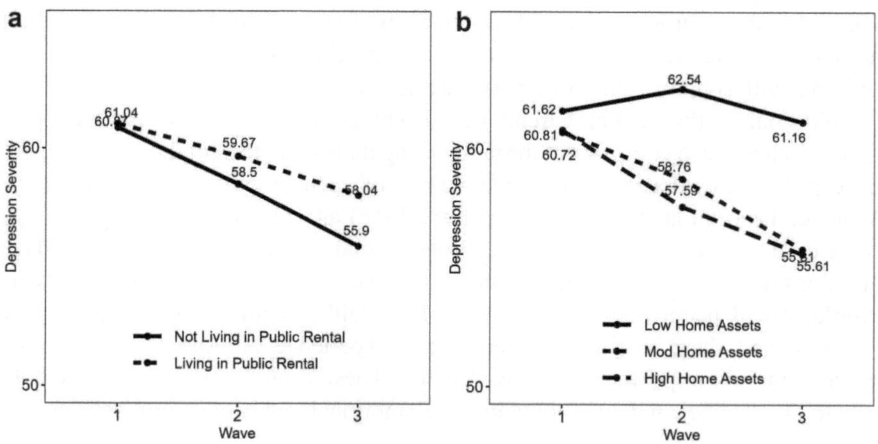

Fig. 4.3 Change in depression severity by housing status and protective home environments

4.4 Summary

Using three-wave longitudinal data from EPYC, this chapter examined the changes in *Depression* and *Depression Severity* over three waves, as well as the risk and protective factors for the baseline level and change in *Depression Severity*.

4.4.1 Depression Improving After Entering the Justice System

Results from the latent growth curve modelling showed that depression-related outcomes in young offenders were, generally, on an improving trend since they were under youth justice supervision, although there were significant variations in the trajectories among them. This declining trend found in the present study is consistent with some previous studies (Baker et al., 2022; Sheidow et al., 2008). The potential reasons cited for such a decline in *Depression Severity* over time include age (e.g., levels of depression drop with age), check-ins through research study participation (e.g., more contact with people), interventions received, and the co-occurring mechanisms of emotional and behavioural problems. For example, one hypothesis is that because of the decrease in conduct problems while serving their orders, the emotional problems also decrease (Sheidow et al., 2008).

The declining trend is also consistent with the general strain theory (Agnew, 2006), in that stress leads to heightened negative emotions, which in turn manifests as behavioural problems. For example, it was found that the symptoms of general depression predicted committing assault for both males and females (Tisak et al., 2021). In other words, the level of negative emotions such as depression is highest around the time when the youth committed a crime. After that, offenders will improve with support from the supervising agencies.

Additionally, this declining trend may also highlight the effectiveness of the programmes that these youths went through during their sentence. Studies in Singapore have provided evidence on the effectiveness of such programmes, including the Violence Prevention Program (Zhou et al., 2018) and Functional Family Therapy (Gan et al., 2021; Gan et al., 2019). When offenders are taught ways to manage emotions and de-escalate conflicts more effectively and prosocial ways of solving problems and better decision-making skills, healthy family functioning may be restored, and these young offenders could experience reduced stress, lowered aggression, and improved mental well-being. These programmes could have contributed to declines in depression and other emotional and behavioural problems as shown in this chapter and Chap. 5.

4.4.2 Personality, Violence Exposure, and Housing Status Are Risk Factors for Depression

The most significant predictor of higher depression severity is *Neuroticism*, which is the personality disposition to experience negative affect. *Ceteris paribus*, a one-point increase in *Neuroticism*, is associated with 7.57-point increase in *Depression Severity* at baseline. This is a strong association given the clinically significant change score is estimated to be 10.8.[1] Young offenders with high *Neuroticism* also had higher *Depression Severity* at all three waves. This between-individual effect is supported by numerous studies. A meta-analysis found a strong link between mental illnesses and personality (Kotov et al., 2010). Of all personality traits, neuroticism had the strongest link to almost all mental disorders, including major depressive disorder, unipolar depression, and dysthymic disorder. Despite findings showing personality as a stable trait, there are growing number of studies providing preliminary support that interventions can address temperamental vulnerabilities (Barlow et al., 2014). As neuroticism is a shared vulnerability for many mental disorders, prioritising such a common temperamental mechanism may increase the likelihood of simultaneous improvement across co-occurring disorders with reduced number of treatments (Sauer-Zavala et al., 2017).

Besides neuroticism, this study also found that all types of childhood violence exposures were significantly associated with both higher baseline *Depression Severity* and the follow-up scores. Past studies have shown that early violence exposure may disrupt emotional and cognitive development, lead to trauma-related symptoms, and jeopardise the development of stress-regulating systems (Mueller & Tronick, 2019). This may in turn increase the risk of lifelong health problems (Moffitt, 2013), clinically significant emotional disorders (Briggs-Gowan et al., 2012; Mandelli et al., 2015), and antisocial behaviours later in life (Wilson et al., 2009). Prevention methods aimed to reduce early violence exposure such as Triple P and interventions to treat violence-related trauma such as trauma-focused CBT programmes were found to be effective in different settings (Lenz & Hollenbaugh, 2015; Nowak & Heinrichs, 2008).

Another important risk factor is the housing status of young offenders. Housing status represented the socio-economic status of these youths and their families. The findings showed that those who lived in public rental housing had less improvement in depression, resulting in a larger gap in *Depression Severity* by Wave 3, despite the fact that their baseline *Depression Severity* was almost equal to those who did not live in rental housing. This finding adds to the current literature which showed evidence that young offenders from such households face multiple disadvantages. It was found that residence in public rental housing is associated with higher hospital utilisation, higher risk of depression, and an increased risk of all-cause mortality

[1] Reliable change index is estimated based on a standard error of 8.5 and reliability of 0.79 for this scale.

(Low et al., 2016; Seng et al., 2018; Wee et al., 2014). These findings justify extra support for these youths from lower socio-economic backgrounds, such as access to early health and mental health screening services.

4.4.3 Family Environment Matters Most

In this study, *Assets* from home, school, and peers all showed significant protective effects towards *Depression Severity* when analysed separately. After adjusting for all covariates, *Protective Assets from the Home Environment* remained as the only significant protective factor. Young offenders with higher baseline *Home Assets* showed more improvement in depression over time. For those with low *Home Assets*, their depression levels did not change for the better over time. The results also suggested that moderate levels of protection from the home environment were good enough to alleviate depressive symptomatology. Therefore, increasing protective factors within the family environment from a low to at least a moderate level should be the target of interventions. Due to the importance of family protective factors, we will analyse in more detail on the relationship between changes in such factors and changes in EBPs in Chap. 7.

References

Achenbach, T. M. (2001). *Manual for ASEBA school-age forms & profiles*. University of Vermont, Research Center for Children, Youth & Families.

Agnew, R. (2006). General strain theory: Current status and directions for further research. In F. T. Cullen, J. P. Wright, & K. R. Blevins (Eds.), *Taking stock: The status of criminological theory* (pp. 101–123). Transaction Publishers.

Alves Donato, A. N., Waclawovsky, A. J., Tonello, L., Firth, J., Smith, L., Stubbs, B., Schuch, F. B., & Boullosa, D. (2021). Association between cardiorespiratory fitness and depressive symptoms in children and adolescents: A systematic review and meta-analysis. *Journal of Affective Disorders, 282*, 1234–1240. https://doi.org/10.1016/j.jad.2021.01.032

Baek, H., Roberts, A. M., & Higgins, G. E. (2019). The impact of negative stimuli on suicidality among adulthoods: A mediating effect of depression. *Deviant Behavior, 40*(7), 778–790. https://doi.org/10.1080/01639625.2018.1438823

Baker, A. E., Padgaonkar, N. T., Galván, A., Frick, P. J., Steinberg, L., & Cauffman, E. (2022). Characterizing trajectories of anxiety, depression, and criminal offending in male adolescents over the 5 years following their first arrest. *Development and Psychopathology*, 1–17. https://doi.org/10.1017/s0954579421001723

Barlow, D. H., Sauer-Zavala, S., Carl, J. R., Bullis, J. R., & Ellard, K. K. (2014). The nature, diagnosis, and treatment of neuroticism: Back to the future. *Clinical Psychological Science, 2*(3), 344–365. https://doi.org/10.1177/2167702613505532

Baskin, D., & Sommers, I. (2015). Trajectories of exposure to community violence and mental health symptoms among serious adolescent offenders. *Criminal Justice and Behavior, 42*(6), 587–609. https://doi.org/10.1177/0093854814556882

Beaudry, G., Yu, R. Q., Langstrom, N., & Fazel, S. (2021). An updated systematic review and meta-regression analysis: Mental disorders among adolescents in juvenile detention and correctional facilities. *Journal of the American Academy of Child and Adolescent Psychiatry, 60*(1), 46–60. https://doi.org/10.1016/j.jaac.2020.01.015

Bernard, J. (2018). Depression: A review of its definition. *MOJ Addiction Medicine & Therapy, 5*(1), 6–7. https://doi.org/10.15406/mojamt.2018.05.00082

Bodden, D. H. M., Stikkelbroek, Y., & Dirksen, C. D. (2018). Societal burden of adolescent depression, an overview and cost-of-illness study. *Journal of Affective Disorders, 241*, 256–262. https://doi.org/10.1016/j.jad.2018.06.015

Briggs-Gowan, M. J., Carter, A. S., & Ford, J. D. (2012). Parsing the effects violence exposure in early childhood: Modeling developmental pathways. *Journal of Pediatric Psychology, 37*(1), 11–22. https://doi.org/10.1093/jpepsy/jsr063

Burlaka, V., Hong, J. S., Churakova, I., Serdiuk, O., Proskura, V., & Shvets, D. (2020). The role of adverse childhood experiences and corporal punishment in early adulthood depression and substance use among Ukrainian college students. *Journal of Family Violence, 35*(3), 285–295. https://doi.org/10.1007/s10896-019-00110-x

Clements-Nolle, K., & Waddington, R. (2019). Adverse childhood experiences and psychological distress in juvenile offenders: The protective influence of resilience and youth assets. *Journal of Adolescent Health, 64*(1), 49–55. https://doi.org/10.1016/j.jadohealth.2018.09.025

da Silva, M. C., Cruz, A. P. M., & Teixeira, M. O. (2021). Depression, anxiety, and drug usage history indicators among institutionalized juvenile offenders of Brasilia. *Psicologia-Reflexao E Critica, 34*(1), 17. https://doi.org/10.1186/s41155-021-00184-x

Domalanta, D. D., Risser, W. L., Roberts, R. E., & Risser, J. M. H. (2003). Prevalence of depression and other psychiatric disorders among incarcerated youths. *Journal of the American Academy of Child and Adolescent Psychiatry, 42*(4), 477–484. https://doi.org/10.1097/01.Chi.0000046819.95464.0b

Gaete, J., Labbe, N., del Villar, P., Allende, C., Araya, R., & Valenzuela, E. (2018). Mental health and associated factors among young offenders in Chile: A cross-sectional study. *Criminal Behaviour and Mental Health, 28*(1), 13–27. https://doi.org/10.1002/cbm.2029

Gan, D. Z. Q., Zhou, Y., Hoo, E., Chong, D., & Chu, C. M. (2019). The implementation of functional family therapy (FFT) as an intervention for youth probationers in Singapore. *Journal of Marital and Family Therapy, 45*(4), 684–698. https://doi.org/10.1111/jmft.12353

Gan, D. Z., Zhou, Y., Abdul Wahab, N. D. B., Ruby, K., & Hoo, E. (2021). Effectiveness of functional family therapy in a non-western context: Findings from a randomized-controlled evaluation of youth offenders in Singapore. *Family Process, 60*(4), 1170–1184. https://doi.org/10.1111/famp.12630

Gover, A. R. (2004). Childhood sexual abuse, gender, and depression among incarcerated youth. *International Journal of Offender Therapy and Comparative Criminology, 48*(6), 683–696. https://doi.org/10.1177/0306624x04264459

Gover, A. R., & MacKenzie, D. L. (2003). Child maltreatment and adjustment to Juvenile correctional institutions. *Criminal Justice and Behavior, 30*(3), 374–396. https://doi.org/10.1177/0093854803030003006

Heller, P., Morosan, L., Badoud, D., Laubscher, M., Olariaga, L. J., Debbane, M., Wolff, H., & Baggio, S. (2022). Prevalence rates and evolution of psychiatric disorders among incarcerated youths in comparison with non-incarcerated youths. *Frontiers in Psychiatry, 12*, 784954. https://doi.org/10.3389/fpsyt.2021.784954

Hinduja, S., & Patchin, J. W. (2010). Bullying, cyberbullying, and suicide. *Archives of Suicide Research, 14*(3), 206–221. https://doi.org/10.1080/13811118.2010.494133

Holzer, K. J., Oh, S., Salas-Wright, C. P., Vaughn, M. G., & Landess, J. (2018). Gender differences in the trends and correlates of major depressive episodes among juvenile offenders in the United States. *Comprehensive Psychiatry, 80*, 72–80. https://doi.org/10.1016/j.comppsych.2017.09.005

Huang, C. C., Chen, Y. F., & Cheung, S. (2021). Early childhood exposure to intimate partner violence and teen depression symptoms in the US. *Health and Social Care in the Community, 29*(5), 47–55. https://doi.org/10.1111/hsc.13240

Jencks, J. W., & Leibowitz, G. S. (2018). The impact of types and extent of trauma on depressive affect among male juvenile sexual offenders. *International Journal of Offender Therapy and Comparative Criminology, 62*(5), 1143–1163. https://doi.org/10.1177/0306624x16676099

Kenny, D. T., Lennings, C. J., & Munn, O. A. (2008). Risk factors for self-harm and suicide in incarcerated young offenders: Implications for policy and practice. *Journal of Forensic Psychology Practice, 8*(4), 358–382. https://doi.org/10.1080/15228930802199317

Kotov, R., Gamez, W., Schmidt, F., & Watson, D. (2010). Linking "big" personality traits to anxiety, depressive, and substance use disorders: A meta-analysis. *Psychological Bulletin, 136*(5), 768–821. https://doi.org/10.1037/a0020327

Larsen, R. (2011). Missing data imputation versus full information maximum likelihood with second-level dependencies. *Structural Equation Modeling, 18*(4), 649–662. https://doi.org/10.1080/10705511.2011.607721

Lenz, A. S., & Hollenbaugh, K. M. (2015). Meta-analysis of trauma-focused cognitive behavioral therapy for treating PTSD and co-occurring depression among children and adolescents. *Counseling Outcome Research and Evaluation, 6*(1), 18–32. https://doi.org/10.1177/2150137815573790

Low, L. L., Wah, W., Ng, M. J., Tan, S. Y., Liu, N., & Lee, K. H. (2016). Housing as a social determinant of health in Singapore and its association with readmission risk and increased utilization of hospital services. *Frontiers in Public Health, 4*, 109. https://doi.org/10.3389/fpubh.2016.00109

Lyu, S. Y., Chi, Y. C., Farabee, D., Tsai, L. T., Lee, M. B., Lo, F. E., & Morisky, D. E. (2015). Psychological distress in an incarcerated Juvenile population. *Journal of the Formosan Medical Association, 114*(11), 1076–1081. https://doi.org/10.1016/j.jfma.2014.03.011

Mandelli, L., Petrelli, C., & Serretti, A. (2015). The role of specific early trauma in adult depression: A meta-analysis of published literature. Childhood trauma and adult depression. *European Psychiatry: The Journal of the Association of European Psychiatrists, 30*(6), 665–680. https://doi.org/10.1016/j.eurpsy.2015.04.007

Matsuura, N., Hashimoto, T., & Toichi, M. (2013). Associations among adverse childhood experiences, aggression, depression, and self-esteem in serious female juvenile offenders in Japan. *The Journal of Forensic Psychiatry & Psychology, 24*(1), 111–127. https://doi.org/10.1080/14789949.2012.746384

Moffitt, T. E. (2013). Childhood exposure to violence and lifelong health: Clinical intervention science and stress-biology research join forces. *Development and Psychopathology, 25*, 1619–1634. https://doi.org/10.1017/S0954579413000801

Mueller, I., & Tronick, E. (2019). Early life exposure to violence: Developmental consequences on brain and behavior. *Frontiers in Behavioral Neuroscience, 13*, 156. https://doi.org/10.3389/fnbeh.2019.00156

National Academies of Sciences, Engineering, and Medicine. (2022). The limits of recidivism: Measuring success after prison. Washington, DC: The National Academies Press. https://doi.org/10.17226/26459

Nowak, C., & Heinrichs, N. (2008). A comprehensive meta-analysis of triple P-positive parenting program using hierarchical linear modeling: Effectiveness and moderating variables. *Clinical Child and Family Psychology Review, 11*(3), 114–144. https://doi.org/10.1007/s10567-008-0033-0

Ozkan, T., Rocque, M., & Posick, C. (2019). Reconsidering the link between depression and crime: A longitudinal assessment. *Criminal Justice and Behavior, 46*(7), 961–979. https://doi.org/10.1177/0093854818799811

Pengpid, S., & Peltzer, K. (2020). Prevalence and associated factors of child abuse and its effects on anxiety and depression among children in Sierra Leone: Results of the 2017 multiple indicator cluster survey. *Journal of Psychology in Africa, 30*(5), 466–470. https://doi.org/10.1080/14330237.2020.1821982

Sauer-Zavala, S., Wilner, J. G., & Barlow, D. H. (2017). Addressing neuroticism in psychological treatment. *Personality Disorders, 8*(3), 191–198. https://doi.org/10.1037/per0000224

Semenza, D. C., & Link, N. W. (2019). How does reentry get under the skin? Cumulative reintegration barriers and health in a sample of recently incarcerated men. *Social Science & Medicine, 243*, 112618. https://doi.org/10.1016/j.socscimed.2019.112618

Seng, J. J. B., Kwan, Y. H., Goh, H., Thumboo, J., & Low, L. L. (2018). Public rental housing and its association with mortality – A retrospective, cohort study. *BMC Public Health, 18*(1), 665. https://doi.org/10.1186/s12889-018-5583-6

Sheidow, A. J., Strachan, M. K., Minden, J. A., Henry, D. B., Tolan, P. H., & Gorman-Smith, D. (2008). The relation of antisocial behavior patterns and changes in internalizing symptoms for a sample of inner-city youth: Comorbidity within a developmental framework. *Journal of Youth and Adolescence, 37*(7), 821–829. https://doi.org/10.1007/s10964-007-9265-4

Southwick, S. M., & Charney, D. S. (2012). The science of resilience: Implications for the prevention and treatment of depression , 338(6103), 79–82. https://doi.org/10.1126/science.1222942.

Tisak, J., Tisak, M. S., Baker, E. R., Amrhein, K. E., & Jensen, C. (2021). The association among parental bonding, depression, social aggression, and criminal assault: Are there gender differences between male and female youth offenders? *Journal of Interpersonal Violence, 36*(3–4), 1883–1908. https://doi.org/10.1177/0886260517744192

Twenge, J. M., Cooper, A. B., Joiner, T. E., Duffy, M. E., & Binau, S. G. (2019). Age, period, and cohort trends in mood disorder indicators and suicide-related outcomes in a nationally representative dataset, 2005–2017. *Journal of Abnormal Psychology, 128*(3), 185–199. https://doi.org/10.1037/abn0000410

van Geel, M., Vedder, P., & Tanilon, J. (2014). Relationship between peer victimization, cyberbullying, and suicide in children and adolescents: A meta-analysis. *JAMA Pediatrics, 168*(5), 435–442. https://doi.org/10.1001/jamapediatrics.2013.4143

Wanklyn, S. G., Day, D. M., Hart, T. A., & Girard, T. A. (2012). Cumulative childhood maltreatment and depression among incarcerated youth: Impulsivity and hopelessness as potential intervening variables. *Child Maltreatment, 17*(4), 306–317. https://doi.org/10.1177/1077559512466956

Wee, L. E., Yong, Y. Z., Chng, M. W. X., Chew, S. H., Cheng, L., Chua, Q. H. A., Yek, J. J. L., Lau, L. J. F., Anand, P., Hoe, J. T. M., Shen, H. M., & Koh, G. C.-H. (2014). Individual and area-level socioeconomic status and their association with depression amongst community-dwelling elderly in Singapore. *Aging & Mental Health, 18*(5), 628–641. https://doi.org/10.1080/13607863.2013.866632

Wilson, H. W., Stover, C. S., & Berkowitz, S. J. (2009). Research review: The relationship between childhood violence exposure and juvenile antisocial behavior: A meta-analytic review. *Journal of Child Psychology and Psychiatry, and Allied Disciplines, 50*(7), 769–779. https://doi.org/10.1111/j.1469-7610.2008.01974.x

World Health Organization. (2021). *Adolescent mental health* [Fact sheet]. https://www.who.int/news-room/fact-sheets/detail/adolescent-mental-health

Yeatts, P. E., Martin, S. B., & Petrie, T. A. (2017). Physical fitness as a moderator of neuroticism and depression in adolescent boys and girls. *Personality and Individual Differences, 114*, 30–35. https://doi.org/10.1016/j.paid.2017.03.040

Zhou, J., Witt, K., Zhang, Y., Chen, C., Qiu, C., Cao, L., & Wang, X. (2014). Anxiety, depression, impulsivity and substance misuse in violent and non-violent adolescent boys in detention in China. *Psychiatry Research, 216*(3), 379–384. https://doi.org/10.1016/j.psychres.2014.01.024

Zhou, Y. Q., Gan, D. Z. Q., Hoo, E. C. C., Chong, D., & Chu, C. M. (2018). Evaluating the violence prevention program: Group and individual changes in aggression, anger, self-control, and empathy. *Journal of Forensic Psychiatry & Psychology, 29*(2), 265–287. https://doi.org/10.1080/14789949.2017.1375541

Chapter 5
Drug Use in Young Offenders: The Link to Emotional and Behavioural Problems

Carl Yeo and Eric Hoo

Contents

Emotional and behavioural problems (EBPs) along with drug use interrupt adolescent milestones, a critical period for youth development (Collishaw, 2015; Glei et al., 2020; United Nations Office on Drugs and Crime, 2018). Young offenders are especially affected during their developmental period as they have higher rates of these problems than the general youth population. Estimates show that up to 61.7% of these youths have some EBPs compared to 14% of the general youth population (Beaudry et al., 2021; World Health Organization, 2021). Rates of drug use are similarly higher in young offenders at 34–86% (Vaughn et al., 2005; Wasserman et al., 2010) compared to 3–30% in the general youth population (UNODC, 2018). It is no surprise then that co-occurring EBPs and drug use are common in these youths. Around 25–65% of them are estimated to have co-occurring problems (Abram et al., 2003; Borges et al., 2018; Hussey et al., 2007; Kim et al., 2017). Indeed, the high proportion is worrying because young offenders with co-occurring

C. Yeo (✉) · E. Hoo
National Council of Social Service, Singapore, Singapore
e-mail: carl_yeo@ncss.gov.sg

D. Li et al. (eds.), *Emotional and Behavioural Problems of Young Offenders in Singapore*, SpringerBriefs in Criminology,
https://doi.org/10.1007/978-3-031-41702-3_5

problems relapse faster and at higher rates (Grella et al., 2001; Schellekens et al., 2015; Tomlinson et al., 2004). Co-occurring EBPs and drug use complicate the already difficult journey these youths face in achieving successful rehabilitation.

The relationship between EBPs and drugs can be conceptualised in three ways (Lehman et al., 1989). First, EBPs are the primary issue and drugs are used to cope with existing problems (self-medication; Khantzian, 1997). Second, drugs are the primary problem and EBPs develop because of drug use. Third, EBPs and drug use share a common underlying cause (e.g., genetic, psychological).

Most research comparing drugs or EBPs as the primary problem have found support for the self-medication hypothesis. They showed that EBPs occurred before drug use (Borges et al., 2018; Kushner et al., 2008; Weiss et al., 2004). However, one argument against self-medication is that not all EBPs are clearly associated with drug use. Prior studies show mixed evidence for emotional problems and drug use but strong support for behavioural problems (Goodman, 2010). Emotional problems focus on symptoms directed inwardly and include problems with anxiety, depression, and somatic symptoms. Behavioural problems focus on symptoms directed outwardly and include problems with impulsivity, disruptive conduct, and substance use. If drugs are used to self-medicate, all types of EBPs should increase the risk of drug use. Therefore, more research is needed to clarify the relationship between EBPs and drug use.

This chapter focuses on understanding co-occurring EBPs and drug use in young offenders using three waves of longitudinal data from the EPYC study. We teased apart the relationship by distinguishing between emotional and behavioural problems. The aim is to understand if these problems increase the risk of drug use, while also testing the converse relationship – drug use increases the risk of EBPs. Additionally, we examine changes in the prevalence of EBPs and drug use.

In this study, participants were coded as using drugs in that wave if they had any drug use in the past 12 months. Drugs were defined as any illegal substances under Singapore's Misuse of Drugs Act (MDA). Enacted in 1973, the MDA is the law that regulates dangerous and harmful substances by specifying which substances are controlled, the associated penalties, along with treatment and rehabilitation of drug abusers (Misuse of Drugs Act, 1973). Illegal substances include cannabis, heroin, methamphetamine, and other common harmful substances. EBPs were measured in two broad categories: emotional problems and behavioural problems. These were measured using the syndrome scale in the Youth Self-Report for ages 11 to 18 years (YSR; Achenbach & Rescorla, 2001) and Adult Self-Report for ages 19 years and above (ASR; Achenbach & Rescorla, 2001). Specific EBPs were measured using the DSM-oriented scale. Anxiety problems, attention-deficit hyperactivity problems (ADHD), depression, and somatic problems were measured in both YSR and ASR. However, conduct problems and oppositional problems were only measured in YSR, while antisocial personality problems were only measured in ASR. More details of this study's methods can be found in Chap. 2.

5.1 Changes in EBPs and Drug Use

The EBPs and drug use among young offenders typically decrease after leaving detention or treatment. For example, Grella et al. (2001) tracked 992 adolescent patients in substance abuse treatment programmes for a year. They found reductions in the use of substances such as alcohol, marijuana, cocaine, hallucinogens, and stimulants. Teplin et al. (2012) examined 1,829 incarcerated juveniles and found that prevalence rates for mental problems declined 5 years after baseline. While much has been done in Western societies, little is known about young offenders in Asian societies. Therefore, we examined how EBPs and drug use changed over time in a group of Singaporean young offenders.

Table 5.1 shows our participants' self-reported EBPs and drug use. At Wave 1, our participants had higher rates of drug use (51.1%) and EBPs (30.3% emotional problems, 54.6% behavioural problems) than the global youth population. The rates are higher than the general youth population with estimates of drug use ranging from 3% to 30% (UNODC, 2018) and mental health rates at 14% (World Health Organization, 2021). Compared to young offenders in other jurisdictions, our participants had generally lower rates of drug use and EBPs. Rates of drug use were reported to be 86.6% in the USA (Vaughn et al., 2005), 62.5% in Austria (Plattner et al., 2012), 88.5% in Nigeria (Olashore et al., 2017), and 53.7% in Germany (Köhler et al., 2009). As described in Chap. 3, our participants had substantially lower rates of EBPs than other countries whose rates ranged from 60% to 93.3%

Table 5.1 EBPs and drug use by data collection wave

	Wave 1 (*n* = 790)	*Wave 2* (*n* = 755)	*Wave 3* (*n* = 598)
Drug use (%)			
Any drug use	51.1	20.0	16.9
Emotional problems (%)			
Any emotional problems	30.3	23.7	9.5
Anxiety problems	7.2	4.6	3.0
Depression	14.6	10.5	6.2
Somatic problems	4.1	4.3	2.7
Behavioural problems (%)			
Any behavioural problems	54.6	34.4	15.4
ADHD	8.0	4.0	4.5
Antisocial personality problems	–	–	10.9[a]
Conduct problems	29.1	15.2	17.7[b]
Oppositional problems	19.6	13.1	12.3[b]

Note: Emotional and behavioural problems were measured by the YSR/ASR syndrome scale, while anxiety problems, depression, somatic problems, ADHD, antisocial personality problems, conduct problems, and oppositional problems were measured by the YSR/ASR DSM-oriented scale. This produced slight differences in overall proportion. Additionally, Wave 3 measures either antisocial personality or conduct and oppositional defiant problems in participants.

[a]Proportion based on 395 participants who did the ASR

[b]Proportion based on 203 participants who did the YSR

(Aida et al., 2014; Fazel et al., 2008). However, this comparison with other jurisdictions should be taken with some caution as these studies differed in measurements of drug use and EBPs. Despite these differences, the results are useful to show a general picture of mental disorder and drug use in the general youth population and in young offenders.

Importantly, the initial rates of EBPs and drug use decreased over time. From Wave 1 to Wave 3, the proportion of youths who used drugs decreased from 51.1% to 16.9%. Similarly, those who reported any emotional problems decreased from 30.3% to 9.5%, while behavioural problems decreased from 54.6% to 15.4%. To exclude the possibility that this decrease was due to sample attrition, we re-examined the results using 543 participants who had data for all three waves, and a similar pattern of decrease was found.

5.2 EBPs and Drug Use

The association between drug use and EBPs is commonly explained by self-medication theory, which states that drugs are used to cope with existing symptoms (Khantzian, 1997). However, not all EBPs are clearly associated with drug use, bringing into question whether self-medication fully explains the relationship between drugs and EBPs.

Behavioural problems are clearly associated with drug use. In a 3-year longitudinal study of 3,607 youths in the UK, behavioural problems predicted subsequent substance use such as alcohol, cannabis, and other illicit drugs (Goodman, 2010). Similar results were found in the USA with a 3-year follow-up (Colder et al., 2013), in Canada with a 3-year follow-up (Henderson et al., 2021), and in Mexico with an 8-year follow-up (Borges et al., 2018). Specific behavioural problems were also associated with drug use. A meta-analysis showed that ADHD and conduct problems were associated with subsequent illicit drug use in youths 18 years or younger with a minimum follow-up period of 2 years (Erskine et al., 2016). Even with a longer follow-up period of 10 years, ADHD was a risk for subsequent drug use (Wilens et al., 2011).

The association between emotional problems and drug use is more ambiguous. Some studies found a positive association between emotional problems and drug use (Borges et al., 2018; Esmaeelzadeh et al., 2018). For example, a review of 36 studies among youths and young adults in the USA and Canada found that depression and anxiety had a positive association with cannabis use (Esmaeelzadeh et al., 2018). Others did not find any association (Goodman, 2010; Henderson et al., 2021; Miettunen et al., 2014). A study on 6,349 participants in Finland with a 15-year follow-up found that behavioural rather than emotional problems were a risk factor for drug use (Miettunen et al., 2014). Similarly, youths with emotional problems had similar substance use disorder severity as those without any EBPs (Henderson et al., 2021). It was youths with either behavioural problems or co-occurring emotional and behavioural problems who had more severe substance use disorders.

Therefore, teasing apart emotional and behavioural problems is important to understand how EBPs and drug use are related.

This section examines the effect of EBPs on drug use in young offenders in Singapore. We contribute to the literature by focusing on the offender population in an Asian society. Additionally, one limitation of past studies is that they examined how EBPs at baseline affected drug use within a follow-up period without considering how EBPs changed over time. In this study, we controlled for changes in EBPs and drug use, and any correlations between emotional and behavioural problems using cross-lagged panel analysis (CLPA). Controlling for these changes using CLPA allows us to determine the effect of EBPs on drug use with greater certainty.

5.2.1 Cross-Lagged Panel Analysis

The CLPA examines how EBPs and drug use influence each other over time (Kearney, 2017; Kuiper & Ryan, 2018). Figure 5.1 shows the CLPA model for this study with relationships between variables represented by arrows.

Key relationships in CLPA are cross-lagged relationships and stability relationships which are represented by solid line arrows. The cross-lagged relationship examines how drug use at Wave 1 affected EBPs at Wave 2 and vice versa. Stability relationships examine how the same variable influences itself over time (e.g., emotional problems at Wave 1 affecting emotional problems at Wave 2).

Correlations between variables are indicated by dotted line arrows. We include correlations between drug use, emotional problems, and behavioural problems. Additionally, longer-lag relationships linking Wave 1 to Wave 3 variables are included as drug relapses do occur over wave periods longer than 1 year (Kassani et al., 2015; Xie et al., 2005). Finally, age, race (Chinese), and sex (female) are included to control for demographic differences. Taken together, the CLPA shows the effect of EBPs on drug use across time and vice versa, while also controlling for changes in EBPs and drug use.

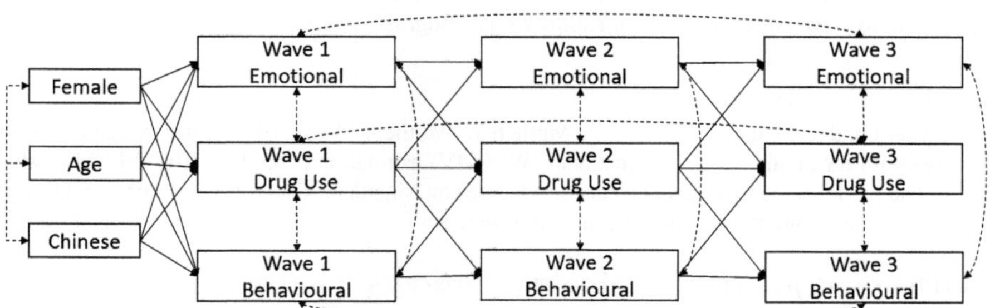

Fig. 5.1 CLPA model with associations between drug use and EBPs
Note: interval between waves is 1 year

5.2.2 Behavioural Problems Increased the Risk of Drug Use

Our CLPA model[1] was a good fit to the data.[2] Behavioural problems increased the risk of drug use, while emotional problems did not. This is shown in Fig. 5.2 with the presence of cross-lagged arrows from Wave 1 behavioural problems to Wave 2 drug use and Wave 2 behavioural problems to Wave 3 drug use. No relationship was found between prior emotional problems and subsequent drug use. Based on the Orth et al. (2022) guidelines, behavioural problems had a medium to large effect on subsequent drug use ($\beta = 0.111$ to 0.114, $p < 0.05$). Additionally, drug use lowered subsequent scores of behavioural problems ($\beta = -0.040$ to -0.078, $p < 0.05$), but no effect was found for emotional problems. We conducted follow-up analyses to examine the relationship between specific emotional problems and drug use. The CLPA model included all variables except that the emotional problem score was changed to either anxiety,[3] depression,[4] or somatic problems.[5] None of the three emotional problems increased the risk of subsequent drug use even though all three models had a generally good fit to the data. These results showed that the relationship between EBPs and drug use is primarily due to behavioural rather than emotional problems.

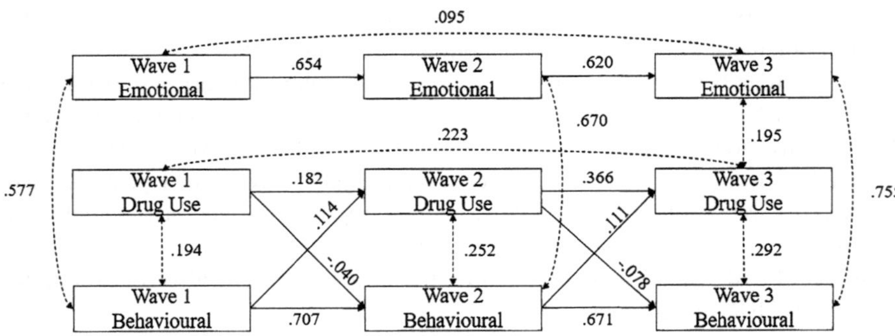

Fig. 5.2 EBPs and drug use
Note: Only statistically significant relationships between emotional problems, behavioural problems, and drug use are shown. Relationships with demographic variables are not shown

[1]Analysis conducted using Mplus 8.7 (Muthén & Muthén, 1998–2017) using weighted least squares with mean and variable adjustment (WLSMV) estimation procedure. The WLSMV estimator can model categorical data and accommodates missing data. There were no missing data on the demographic variables. Equality constraints were set for cross-lagged relationships and stability relationships.

[2]$X^2(17) = 50.413$, $p < 0.001$; CFI = 0.976; TLI = 0.908; RMSEA = 0.049.

[3]$X^2(17) = 65.071$, $p < 0.001$; CFI = 0.964; TLI = 0.862; RMSEA = 0.058.

[4]$X^2(17) = 50.109$, $p < 0.001$; CFI = 0.976; TLI = 0.907; RMSEA = 0.048.

[5]$X^2(17) = 36.516$, $p < 0.01$; CFI = 0.983; TLI = 0.933; RMSEA = 0.037.

Additionally, we found significant relationships between demographic variables and the variables of drug use, emotional problems, and behavioural problems. The risk of Wave 1 drug use was higher in older offenders ($\beta = 0.130$, $p < 0.01$) and female offenders ($\beta = 0.101$, $p < 0.01$). Chinese offenders had a lower risk of Wave 1 drug use ($\beta = -0.253$, $p < 0.001$). There were no differences found in age and sex for emotional problems. However, behavioural problem scores were lower in older offenders ($\beta = -0.130$, $p < 0.01$). Chinese offenders had lower emotional ($\beta = -0.142$, $p < 0.001$) and behavioural problem scores ($\beta = -0.106$, $p < 0.01$).

5.3 Summary

This chapter examined changes in the prevalence of EBPs and drug use using three waves of data from the EPYC study. Importantly, we examined how different categories of EBPs (emotional and behavioural) were associated with drug use.

5.3.1 Decrease in Drug Use and EBPs

Young offenders in Singapore benefitted from rehabilitation in the justice system. As shown in Chap. 4, rates of depression declined as they went through the justice system. This chapter expanded the types of EBPs examined and showed that rates of drug use, and other EBPs had similar declines. These findings are in line with other studies, as a systematic review showed that going through the justice system and treatment had reduced substance use in young offenders (Tripodi & Bender, 2011). For similar youths in the UK, emotional and behavioural symptoms also decreased 6 months after entry into correctional institutions (Lennox et al., 2013). Other studies showed a similar decrease 5 years after entry (Teplin et al., 2012).

One reason for the reduction in rates of EBPs and drug use could be that young offenders attended rehabilitation programmes provided by correctional agencies. While this study did not examine the programmes received by participants, other studies have shown the effectiveness of rehabilitation programmes, especially cognitive-behavioural ones (Redondo et al., 2012). Another reason for the reduction could be the structured routine and support services provided by the justice system. An unhealthy and chaotic environment might be a cause of drug use and EBPs. Therefore, placing young offenders in a secure and stable environment might be another reason for their improvement (Lennox et al., 2013).

5.3.2 Behavioural Problems Associated with Drug Use

In our study, the relationship between drug use and EBPs was driven by behavioural rather than emotional problems. Our findings provide further support for the clear association between behavioural problems and drug use, in line with past studies (Borges et al., 2018; Colder et al., 2013; Erskine et al., 2016; Goodman, 2010; Henderson et al., 2021; Wilens et al., 2011). Unlike other studies (Borges et al., 2018; Esmaeelzadeh et al., 2018), we found no relationship between emotional problems and drug use. One possible reason for this discrepancy is that emotional problems are associated with drug use only when they co-occur with behavioural problems. In other words, without co-occurring behavioural problems, youths with emotional problems do not have a higher risk of drug use. This was seen in our study where emotional problems had no effect on drug use once behavioural problems were accounted for. Chapter 6 also shows that behavioural problems were the main risk factor for re-offending after taking into account re-offending risk. Similarly, Henderson et al. (2021) found that youths with only emotional problems did not have more problematic substance use. Rather, more problematic substance use was found in those with behavioural problems or those with co-occurring emotional and behavioural problems.

In the three ways that EBPs might be related to drug use (Lehman et al., 1989), our results do not support the idea that drugs are the primary cause of EBPs. Drug use did not increase emotional or behavioural problems in our study. Our results partially support the self-medication theory (Khantzian, 1997) that drugs are used to cope with EBPs. We found that behavioural problems are associated with drug use, but no relationship was found for emotional problems and drug use. Other studies have even found that emotional problems *decreased* the risk of drug use (Colder et al., 2013). One reason could be that youths use drugs together with their peers. Youths with purely emotional problems may have smaller peer groups, and this may prevent peer-influenced drug use. Another reason could be that the anxiety and worry common in emotional problems deter these youths from risk-taking behaviours such as substance use. However, the question remains for the self-medication theory on why drugs were used to cope with behavioural problems but not with emotional ones.

Our results are most in line with the idea that behavioural problems and drug use share a common underlying cause. Behavioural problems and drug use could share common risk factors such as risk-taking tendencies, antisocial attitudes, drug peers, and family substance use (Ali et al., 2016; Cleveland et al., 2008). Additionally, the perception that emotional problems are related to drug use could be due to co-occurring emotional and behavioural problems. In other words, other variables, rather than EBPs, are the primary cause of drug use. More research is needed to tease apart the effects of emotional and behavioural problems, and compare risk factors for drug use so that rehabilitation can be made more effective.

5.3.3 Screen and Treat EBPs

EBPs should be identified and treated early even though they might not be the primary cause for drug use. Untreated EBPs hinder effective rehabilitation of the direct causes of drug use. Evidence-based approaches to drug prevention emphasise methods such as motivation for abstinence and coping strategies to deal with cravings (McGovern et al., 2005). These methods require cognitive and social skills, skills which individuals with EBPs often lack. For example, drug abusers with ADHD have a lower attention span and found it harder to complete treatment (Drake et al., 2005; Latimer et al., 2004). Additionally, those with EBPs may have difficulty forming therapeutic relationships which are important for effective treatment (Reedy & Hall, 2008). With drug treatment rendered less effective by their EBPs, these individuals are therefore more likely to go back to drugs. Therefore, early screening and treatment of EBPs is important for effective rehabilitation of drug use. One area for treatment of EBPs is the family. As described in Chaps. 4 and 7, those with higher protective home assets show more improvement in depression over time. Additionally, young offenders with improved family factors show similar improvements in their emotional and behavioural problems.

References

Abram, K. M., Teplin, L. A., McClelland, G. M., & Dulcan, M. K. (2003). Comorbid psychiatric disorders in youth in juvenile detention. *Archives of General Psychiatry, 60*(11), 1097–1108. https://doi.org/10.1001/archpsyc.60.11.1097

Achenbach, T. M., & Rescorla, L. A. (2001). *Manual for the ASEBA school-age forms & profiles*. Research Center for Children, Youth, & Families.

Aida, S. A., Aili, H. H., Manveen, K. S., Salwina, W. I., Subash, K. P., Ng, C. G., & Muhsin, A. Z. M. (2014). Prevalence of psychiatric disorders among juvenile offenders in Malaysian prisons and association with socio-demographic and personal factors. *International Journal of Prisoner Health, 10*(2), 132–143. https://doi.org/10.1108/ijph-06-2013-0029

Ali, A., Carré, A., Hassler, C., Spilka, S., Vanier, A., Barry, C., & Berthoz, S. (2016). Risk factors for substances use and misuse among young people in France: What can we learn from the substance use risk profile scale? *Drug and Alcohol Dependence, 163*, 84–91. https://doi.org/10.1016/j.drugalcdep.2016.03.027

Beaudry, G., Yu, R., Långström, N., & Fazel, S. (2021). An updated systematic review and meta-regression analysis: Mental disorders among adolescents in juvenile detention and correctional facilities. *Journal of the American Academy of Child & Adolescent Psychiatry, 60*(1), 46–60. https://doi.org/10.1016/j.jaac.2020.01.015

Borges, G., Benjet, C., Orozco, R., & Medina-Mora, M. E. (2018). A longitudinal study of reciprocal risk between mental and substance use disorders among Mexican youth. *Journal of Psychiatric Research, 105*, 45–53. https://doi.org/10.1016/j.jpsychires.2018.08.014

Cleveland, M. J., Feinberg, M. E., Bontempo, D. E., & Greenberg, M. T. (2008). The role of risk and protective factors in substance use across adolescence. *Journal of Adolescent Health, 43*(2), 157–164. https://doi.org/10.1016/j.jadohealth.2008.01.015

Colder, C. R., Scalco, M., Trucco, E. M., Read, J. P., Lengua, L. J., Wieczorek, W. F., & Hawk, L. W., Jr. (2013). Prospective associations of internalizing and externalizing problems and their co-occurrence with early adolescent substance use. *Journal of Abnormal Child Psychology, 41*(4), 667–677. https://doi.org/10.1007/s10802-012-9701-0

Collishaw, S. (2015). Annual research review: Secular trends in child and adolescent mental health. *The Journal of Child Psychology and Psychiatry, 56*(3), 370–393. https://doi.org/10.1111/jcpp.12372

Drake, R. E., Wallach, M. A., & McGovern, M. P. (2005). Future directions in preventing relapse to substance abuse among clients with severe mental illnesses. *Psychiatric Services, 56*(10), 1297–1302. https://doi.org/10.1176/appi.ps.56.10.1297

Erskine, H. E., Norman, R. E., Ferrari, A. J., Chan, G. C. K., Copeland, W. E., Whiteford, H. A., & Scott, J. G. (2016). Long-term outcomes of attention-deficit/hyperactivity disorder and conduct disorder: A systematic review and meta-analysis. *Journal of the American Academy of Child & Adolescent Psychiatry, 55*(10), 841–850. https://doi.org/10.1016/j.jaac.2016.06.016

Esmaeelzadeh, S., Moraros, J., Thorpe, L., & Bird, Y. (2018). Examining the association and directionality between mental health disorders and substance use among adolescents and young adults in the U.S. and Canada: A systematic review and meta-analysis. *Journal of Clinical Medicine, 7*(12), 543. https://doi.org/10.3390/jcm7120543

Fazel, S., Doll, H., & Långström, N. (2008). Mental disorders among adolescents in juvenile detention and correctional facilities: A systematic review and metaregression analysis of 25 surveys. *Journal of the American Academy of Child & Adolescent Psychiatry, 47*(9), 1010–1019. https://doi.org/10.1097/CHI.ObO13e31817eecf3

Glei, D. A., Stokes, A., & Weinstein, M. (2020). Changes in mental health, pain, and drug misuse since the mid-1990s: Is there a link? *Social Science & Medicine, 246*, 112789. https://doi.org/10.1016/j.socscimed.2020.112789

Goodman, A. (2010). Substance use and common child mental health problems: Examining longitudinal associations in a British sample. *Addiction, 105*(8), 1484–1496. https://doi.org/10.1111/j.1360-0443.2010.02981.x

Grella, C. E., Hser, Y. I., Joshi, V., & Rounds-Bryant, J. (2001). Drug treatment outcomes for adolescents with comorbid mental and substance use disorders. *The Journal of Nervous and Mental Disease, 189*(6), 384–392. https://doi.org/10.1097/00005053-200106000-00006

Henderson, J. L., Wilkins, L. K., Hawke, L. D., Wang, W., Sanches, M., Brownlie, E. B., & Beitchman, J. H. (2021). Longitudinal emergence of concurrent mental health and substance use concerns in an Ontario school-based sample: The research and action for teens study. *Journal of the Canadian Academy of Child and Adolescent Psychiatry, 30*(4), 249–263. https://www.ncbi.nlm.nih.gov/pmc/articles/PMC8561851/

Hussey, D. L., Drinkard, A. M., & Flannery, D. J. (2007). Comorbid substance use and mental disorders among offending youth. *Journal of Social Work Practice in the Addictions, 7*(1–2), 117–138. https://doi.org/10.1300/J160v07n01_07

Kassani, A., Niazi, M., Hassanzadeh, J., & Menati, R. (2015). Survival analysis of drug abuse relapse in addiction treatment centers. *International Journal of High Risk Behaviors And Addiction, 4*(3), 23402. https://doi.org/10.5812/ijhrba.23402

Kearney, M. W. (2017). The Sage encyclopedia of communication research methods. *Sage*. https://doi.org/10.4135/9781483381411

Khantzian, E. J. (1997). The self-medication hypothesis of substance use disorders: A reconsideration and recent applications. *Harvard Review of Psychiatry., 4*(5), 231–244. https://doi.org/10.3109/10673229709030550

Kim, J. I., Kim, B., Kim, B.-N., Hong, S.-B., Lee, D. W., Chung, J.-Y., Choi, J. Y., Choi, B.-S., Oh, Y.-R., & Youn, M. (2017). Prevalence of psychiatric disorders, comorbidity patterns, and repeat offending among male juvenile detainees in South Korea: A cross-sectional study. *Child and Adolescent Psychiatry and Mental Health, 11*(1), 6. https://doi.org/10.1186/s13034-017-0143-x

Köhler, D., Heinzen, H., Hinrichs, G., & Huchzermeier, C. (2009). The prevalence of mental disorders in a German sample of male incarcerated juvenile offenders. *International Journal of Offender Therapy and Comparative Criminology, 53*(2), 211–227. https://doi.org/10.1177/0306624x07312950

Kuiper, R. M., & Ryan, O. (2018). Drawing conclusions from cross-lagged relationships: Re-considering the role of the time-interval. *Structural Equation Modeling: A Multidisciplinary Journal, 25*(5), 809–823. https://doi.org/10.1080/10705511.2018.1431046

Kushner, M. G., Krueger, R., Frye, B., & Peterson, J. (2008). Epidemiological perspectives on co-occurring anxiety disorder and substance use disorder. In S. H. Stewart & P. J. Conrod (Eds.), *Anxiety and substance use disorders: The vicious cycle of comorbidity* (pp. 3–17). Springer. https://doi.org/10.1007/978-0-387-74290-8_1

Latimer, W. W., Ernst, J., Hennessey, J., Stinchfield, R. D., & Winters, K. C. (2004). Relapse among adolescent drug abusers following treatment: The role of probable ADHD status. *Journal of Child & Adolescent Substance Abuse, 13*(3), 1–16. https://doi.org/10.1300/J029v13n03_01

Lehman, A. F., Myers, C. P., & Corty, E. (1989). Assessment and classification of patients with psychiatric and substance abuse syndromes. *Psychiatric Services, 40*(10), 1019–1025. https://doi.org/10.1176/ps.40.10.1019

Lennox, C., Bell, V., O'Malley, K., Shaw, J., & Dolan, M. (2013). A prospective cohort study of the changing mental health needs of adolescents in custody. *BMJ Open, 3*(3), 002358. https://doi.org/10.1136/bmjopen-2012-002358

McGovern, M. P., Wrisley, B. R., & Drake, R. E. (2005). Relapse of substance use disorder and its prevention among persons with co-occurring disorders. *Psychiatric Services, 56*(10), 1270–1273. https://doi.org/10.1176/appi.ps.56.10.1270

Miettunen, J., Murray, G. K., Jones, P. B., Mäki, P., Ebeling, H., Taanila, A., Joukamaa, M., Savolainen, J., Törmänen, S., Järvelin, M. R., Veijola, J., & Moilanen, I. (2014). Longitudinal associations between childhood and adulthood externalizing and internalizing psychopathology and adolescent substance use. *Psychological Medicine, 44*(8), 1727–1738. https://doi.org/10.1017/s0033291713002328

Misuse of Drugs Act. (1973). https://sso.agc.gov.sg/Act/MDA1973

Muthén, L.K., & Muthén, B.O. (1998–2017). Mplus user's guide. Eighth Edition. Los Angeles, CA: Muthén & Muthén

Olashore, A. A., Akanni, O. O., & Olashore, O. O. (2017). Associate factors of delinquency among incarcerated male juveniles in a Borstal Institution in Nigeria. *International Journal of Forensic Mental Health, 16*(3), 207–214. https://doi.org/10.1080/14999013.2017.1288668

Orth, U., Meier, L. L., Bühler, J. L., Dapp, L. C., Krauss, S., Messerli, D., & Robins, R. W. (2022). Effect size guidelines for cross-lagged effects. *Psychological Methods*. Advance online publication. https://doi.org/10.1037/met0000499

Plattner, B., Giger, J., Bachmann, F., Brühwiler, K., Steiner, H., Steinhausen, H. C., Bessler, C., & Aebi, M. (2012). Psychopathology and offense types in detained male juveniles. *Psychiatry Research, 198*(2), 285–290. https://doi.org/10.1016/j.psychres.2012.02.006

Redondo, S., Martínez-Catena, A., & Andrés-Pueyo, A. (2012). Therapeutic effects of a cognitive-behavioural treatment with juvenile offenders. *European Journal of Psychology Applied to Legal Context, 4*, 159–178. https://www.proquest.com/scholarly-journals/therapeutic-effects-cognitive-behavioural/docview/1140206912/se-2

Reedy, A. R., & Hall, J. A. (2008). Treatment issues with substance use disorder clients who have mood or anxiety disorders. *Mental Health and Substance Use, 1*(1), 44–53. https://doi.org/10.1080/17523280701741738

Schellekens, A. F., de Jong, C. A., Buitelaar, J. K., & Verkes, R. J. (2015). Co-morbid anxiety disorders predict early relapse after inpatient alcohol treatment. *European Psychiatry, 30*(1), 128–136. https://doi.org/10.1016/j.eurpsy.2013.08.006

Teplin, L. A., Welty, L. J., Abram, K. M., Dulcan, M. K., & Washburn, J. J. (2012). Prevalence and persistence of psychiatric disorders in youth after detention: A prospective longitudinal study. *Archives of General Psychiatry, 69*(10), 1031–1043. https://doi.org/10.1001/archgenpsychiatry.2011.2062

Tomlinson, K. L., Brown, S. A., & Abrantes, A. (2004). Psychiatric comorbidity and substance use treatment outcomes of adolescents. *Psychology of Addictive Behaviors, 18*(2), 160–169. https://doi.org/10.1037/0893-164X.18.2.160

Tripodi, S. J., & Bender, K. (2011). Substance abuse treatment for juvenile offenders: A review of quasi-experimental and experimental research. *Journal of Criminal Justice, 39*(3), 246–252. https://doi.org/10.1016/j.jcrimjus.2011.02.007

United Nations Office on Drugs and Crime. (2018). *World drug report* (Vol. Sales No. E.18.XI.9). United Nations Publication. https://www.unodc.org/wdr2018/

Vaughn, M. G., Howard, M. O., Foster, K. A., Dayton, M. K., & Zelner, J. L. (2005). Substance use in a state population of incarcerated juvenile offenders. *Journal of Evidence-Based Social Work, 2*(1–2), 155–173. https://doi.org/10.1300/J394v02n01_09

Wasserman, G. A., McReynolds, L. S., Schwalbe, C. S., Keating, J. M., & Jones, S. A. (2010). Psychiatric disorder, comorbidity, and suicidal behavior in juvenile justice youth. *Criminal Justice and Behavior, 37*(12), 1361–1376. https://doi.org/10.1177/0093854810382751

Weiss, R. D., Kolodziej, M., Griffin, M. L., Najavits, L. M., Jacobson, L. M., & Greenfield, S. F. (2004). Substance use and perceived symptom improvement among patients with bipolar disorder and substance dependence. *Journal of Affective Disorders, 79*(1–3), 279–283. https://doi.org/10.1016/s0165-0327(02)00454-8

Wilens, T. E., Martelon, M., Joshi, G., Bateman, C., Fried, R., Petty, C., & Biederman, J. (2011). Does ADHD predict substance-use disorders? A 10-year follow-up study of young adults with ADHD. *Journal of the American Academy of Child & Adolescent Psychiatry, 50*(6), 543–553. https://doi.org/10.1016/j.jaac.2011.01.021

World Health Organization. (2021). *Adolescent mental health*. https://www.who.int/news-room/fact-sheets/detail/adolescent-mental-health

Xie, H., McHugo, G. J., Fox, M. B., & Drake, R. E. (2005). Special section on relapse prevention: Substance abuse relapse in a ten-year prospective follow-up of clients with mental and substance use disorders. *Psychiatric Services, 56*(10), 1282–1287. https://doi.org/10.1176/appi.ps.56.10.1282

Chapter 6
Predicting 2-Year Re-offending Among Young Offenders Under Community Supervision

Carl Yeo and Dongdong Li

Contents

Re-offending is a problem in youths with emotional and behavioural problems (EBPs). Studies show that these youths are at higher risk of re-offending (Basto-Pereira & Farrington, 2022; Wibbelink et al., 2017; Yukhnenko et al., 2020), have higher probation noncompliance (Brooker et al., 2020), as well as a higher likelihood of persistent offending well into adulthood (Remschmidt & Walter, 2010). Despite the potential association with re-offending, EBPs are not included as a major criminogenic need (i.e., factors that are directly related to re-offending) in risk assessment tools such as the Youth Level of Service/Case Management Inventory (YLS/CMI; Hoge & Andrews, 2011). This is because the authors argue that EBPs are factors unique to individuals and how they respond to intervention programmes

C. Yeo (✉) · D. Li
National Council of Social Service, Singapore, Singapore
e-mail: carl_yeo@ncss.gov.sg

D. Li et al. (eds.), *Emotional and Behavioural Problems of Young Offenders in Singapore*, SpringerBriefs in Criminology,
https://doi.org/10.1007/978-3-031-41702-3_6

(Andrews et al., 2011). EBPs are therefore responsivity factors that must be taken into consideration when providing interventions for major criminogenic needs.

Criminogenic needs are more important predictors for re-offending compared to EBPs (Basto-Pereira & Farrington, 2022). However, few studies have examined the effects of EBPs, along with YLS/CMI risk assessment, on re-offending. Additionally, not much is known about whether assessing EBPs will improve the predictive validity of the YLS/CMI. Finally, there is also a lack of studies on Asian young offenders. One of the few comparative analyses showed differences between youths in Western and Asian societies. Compared to young offenders in Brisbane, Australia, those in Shanghai, China committed a smaller variety of offences and had higher rates of committing crimes together with friends (Wei et al., 2004). The authors proposed that the differences arose from greater integration into the family network and community support of young offenders in China. Given the scarcity of research in this area, we have three main aims for this chapter. First, we describe the rates of re-offending in young offenders, their Level of Risk as measured by YLS/CMI 2.0, as well as the prevalence of EBPs to provide statistics on a non-Western population. Second, we examine the associations between the Level of Risk, EBPs, and the re-offending rate. Finally, we investigate whether EBPs provide any incremental predictive ability for re-offending over the YLS/CMI.

Our study used a subsample of the EPYC sample. We examined 545 young offenders under community supervision. These youths were tracked for at least 2 years upon entry into the justice system. The majority of them (80.4%) were sentenced with probation orders, and the rest had a community supervised drug order for first time young drug users. This community sample consisted of 81.8% male and 64.2% non-Chinese and had an average age of 17.4 years at baseline.

6.1 Re-offending, Level of Risk, and EBPs in the Community Sample

6.1.1 Re-offending Rate

The re-offending rate is a common indicator of rehabilitation success across many jurisdictions although each jurisdiction has its own definition of re-offending. In this chapter, participants were coded as re-offended if their sentence was revoked or if they committed offences that resulted in a new sentence within 2 years of the start of their index offence – the offence which led to participation in the EPYC study. Among these young offenders under community supervision, the overall 2-year re-offending rate is 23.9%, with 130 out of the 545 youths re-offended in the follow-up period (Table 6.1). This is similar to the noncompletion rate of probation orders at 22% in a previous Singapore study (Li et al., 2019). Additionally, male and female youths did not differ in their re-offending rates.

Compared to similar samples in the other countries, the re-offending rate among our community sample is substantially lower. For example, an official report from the Texas Juvenile Justice Department showed the 2-year re-offending rate after a

Table 6.1 Descriptive statistics of YLS Level of Risk, emotional, behavioural, and any EBPs

	Female ($n = 99$) (%)	Male ($n = 446$) (%)	Total ($n = 545$) (%)
Re-offending rate[a]	23.2	24.0	23.9
YLS/CMI Level of Risk			
Low-Risk	16.2	10.3	11.4
Moderate-Risk	40.4	50.2	48.4
High-Risk	43.4	39.5	40.2
EBPs			
Any	44.4	45.1	45.0
Emotional problems			
Any emotional problems	22.2	17.0	18.0
Depression	20.2	12.8	14.1
Anxiety problems	5.1	4.7	4.8
Somatic problems	3.0	4.3	4.0
Behavioural problems			
Any behavioural problems	38.4	39.0	38.9
ADHD	9.1	6.3	6.8
Oppositional problems	12.1	17.5	16.5
Conduct problems	21.2	28.3	27.0
Substance dependence	15.2	8.7	9.9

[a]Re-offending refers to any revocation of sentence or any committed offences that resulted in a new sentence within 2 years of the start of their index offence

court order to be 41.6% (Texas Juvenile Justice Department, 2018). Young offenders in New Zealand had a re-offending rate of 67.9% with a tracking period of 2 years after a court order (Ministry of Justice, 2018b). Other studies which tracked 2 years after the completion of a community sentence had similarly higher rates than our Singaporean youths. These ranged from 35.0% in Canada (McCarter, 2012) and 50.0% in Australia (Australian Institute of Health and Welfare, 2018) to 64.6% in England and Wales (Ministry of Justice, 2018a).

6.1.2 Level of Risk

Structured risk assessment, such as the YLS/CMI (Hoge & Andrews, 2011), is widely used across the world to predict re-offending risk and to guide supervision and treatment (Chua et al., 2014; Morgan et al., 2020; Ting et al., 2017). In this study, the Level of Risk was also measured by the YLS/CMI 2.0, an empirically validated tool for assessing re-offending risk (Chu et al., 2015, 2014; Olver et al., 2012; Schwalbe, 2007). The major criminogenic needs from eight domains were summed into a total score and categorised into three risk levels. According to the data presented in Table 6.1, the Low-Risk group constituted 11.4% of the sample, while the Moderate-Risk and High-Risk groups comprised 48.4% and 40.2%, respectively. There were no significant differences between sexes in terms of YLS/CMI 2.0 risk levels.

The Level of Risk distribution in this sample is similar to a recent study on youth probationers in Singapore, where about 90% of the youths were of Moderate/High-Risk (Xu et al., 2020). These rates of Moderate/High-Risk cases were much higher compared to another Singapore study using data from a decade ago, in which 55.4% were Moderate-Risk and only 4.0% High-Risk (Chu et al., 2015). This is because more emphasis was placed in recent years on diverting Low-Risk youths away from the criminal justice system. Instead of receiving community sentences, the youths with lower risk were more likely to be placed in diversionary programmes. In other words, agencies dealing with community sentences, such as probation services, have been supervising youths who were assessed as having a higher risk classification in recent years.

6.1.3 EBPs

In terms of EBPs, past studies have consistently revealed two broad categories: inwardly directed emotional problems and outwardly directed behavioural problems (Willner et al., 2016). In this chapter, we examined three emotional problems (anxiety problems, depression, and somatic problems) and four behavioural problems (ADHD, conduct problems, oppositional problems, and substance dependence) in a manner similar to Chap. 3. The study's findings revealed that among young offenders under community sentence, 45.0% exhibited at least one type of EBPs (Table 6.1). Of the sample, 38.9% had behavioural problems and 18.0% had emotional problems. There was no statistically significant difference found between males and females in relation to EBPs.

Compared to the results in Chap. 3 which examined youths under community supervision and in institutions, this community-only sample had a lower prevalence of behavioural problems, especially conduct problems, oppositional problems, and substance dependence. Similar to Chap. 3, female young offenders had higher substance dependence than males.

6.2 EBPs and Level of Risk

Unsurprisingly, young offenders with a higher Level of Risk had more EBPs. As shown in Table 6.2, High-Risk youths had the highest proportion of EBPs (65.3%) compared to Moderate-Risk (32.6%) and Low-Risk (25.8%) youths. The higher EBP rates were also shown in behavioural only problems where High-Risk youths had almost four times those of the Low-Risk youths (42.0% vs 11.3%). Surprisingly, emotional only problems in High-Risk youths were lower than those of Low-Risk

Table 6.2 EBPs in youths at different YLS/CMI levels of risk

	YLS/CMI Level of Risk		
	Low-Risk (n = 62) (%)	Moderate-Risk (n = 264) (%)	High-Risk (n = 219) (%)
EBPs	25.8	32.6	65.3
Behavioural only	11.3	18.2	42.0
Emotional only	11.3	5.7	5.0
Comorbid	3.2	8.7	18.3

youths (5.0% vs 11.3%). This does not mean that High-Risk youths did not have emotional problems, but their emotional problems were commonly comorbid with behavioural problems. Rates of comorbid problems in High-Risk youths were almost six times those of Low-Risk youths (18.3% vs 3.2%). This is worrying, as young offenders with comorbid problems are at higher risk of persistent re-offending not just during adolescence (McReynolds et al., 2010) but well into their young adult years (Hoeve et al., 2013).

6.3 Re-offending Rates Based on Level of Risk and EBPs

To date, there has been limited research examining the combined effects of EBPs and Level of Risk on re-offending rates of young offenders. Past studies have established a clear link between the YLS/CMI Level of Risk and re-offending (Basto-Pereira et al., 2021; Hilterman et al., 2014; Onifade et al., 2008). For example, Chu et al. (2015) found that the YLS/CMI 2.0 predicted re-offending for both sexes in a study of 3,264 youths in Singapore who have offended. Similarly, EBPs have also been associated with re-offending (Hein et al., 2017; McReynolds et al., 2010; Wibbelink et al., 2017). EBPs contributed to re-offending within a year of release in a sample of 11,557 male youths under long-term custody (Baglivio et al., 2017). However, few studies have examined the impact of both EBPs and Level of Risk on re-offending rates of young offenders, highlighting the need for further research in this area.

We found that, among youths of the same Level of Risk, those with EBPs had higher re-offending rates than those without (Table 6.3). Additionally, High-Risk youths with EBPs had the highest re-offending rate and Low-Risk youths without EBPs had the lowest re-offending rate ($\chi2$ [5] = 38.50, $p < 0.001$).

The findings indicate that EBPs, along with Level of Risk, are important predictors of re-offending rates in young offenders. However, as EBPs are not included in YLS/CMI's measure of Level of Risk, we examined the extent to which including EBPs in the YLS/CMI would increase its predictive accuracy.

Table 6.3 Two-year re-offending rates based on level of risk and EBPs

YLS/CMI Level of Risk	EBPs	Sample size	2-year re-offending rates (%)	Group re-offending rates (%)
Low-Risk	Absent	46	0.0	3.2
	Present	16	12.5	
Moderate-Risk	Absent	178	18.5	20.1
	Present	86	23.3	
High-Risk	Absent	76	23.7	34.2
	Present	143	39.9	

6.4 Incremental Validity of EBP Assessment in Predicting Re-offending

To our knowledge, only two studies have examined the incremental validity of EBPs over Level of Risk in predicting re-offending. Guebert and Olver (2014) examined 186 Canadian youths charged with violent offences and found that only substance use problems was predictive of re-offending after controlling for YLS/CMI. Similarly, McCormick et al. (2017) studied 232 youths referred by the courts for EBP assessment and found that youths with treated criminogenic needs had a lower risk of re-offending, while treatment of non-criminogenic EBPs needs had no effect on re-offending. Both studies suggest that EBPs did not have any incremental validity in predicting re-offending over Level of Risk. However, other studies showed that behavioural problems had a stronger association with re-offending than emotional problems. In a meta-analysis of 20 studies from 1995 to 2014, behavioural problems had small to moderate mean effect sizes on re-offending, but no relation was found between emotional problems and re-offending (Wibbelink et al., 2017). In contrast, both emotional and behavioural problems were found to contribute to re-offending in a sample of 11,557 male youths under long-term custody (Baglivio et al., 2017). Given the discrepancies in the previous findings, our study will examine emotional and behavioural problems separately in addition to overall EBPs.

In this study, we conducted logistic regression to examine whether including EBPs would provide additional predictive power for re-offending over Level of Risk while controlling for age, sex, and race. We tested a total of four models. Model 1 was a reference model predicting re-offending using Level of Risk without EBPs. In Models 2–4, different types of EBPs were added to the reference model. Model 2 included EBPs as one general variable. Model 3 examined emotional and behavioural problems as two separate variables. Model 4 examined EBPs as seven specific problems. We tested the incremental predictive validity of EBPs over Level of Risk by comparing models 2–4 with Model 1 on fit indices such as likelihood ratio χ^2 (LCRS), Akaike information criterion (AIC), and Bayesian information criterion (BIC). Better models were indicated by a significant likelihood ratio test along with lower AIC and BIC scores. Additionally, each model's predictive accuracy was shown by their area under the receiver operating characteristic curve (AUC) with higher AUC values indicating better accuracy. To check for multicollinearity, we computed VIF for each variable. All predictor variables had VIF values below 2, well within the guidelines of less than 5 and therefore unlikely to show multicollinearity (Tsagris & Pandis, 2021).

Our logistic regression results are shown in Table 6.4. Consistent with the bivariate analysis, higher Level of Risk was associated with a higher re-offending rate. Moderate and High Level of Risk increased odds of re-offending by 7.62 times and 13.00 times, respectively (Model 1). These relationships remain significant even after including EBP variables in models 2–4.

The findings also showed that the inclusion of EBPs had some incremental validity over Level of Risk in predicting re-offending. Compared to Model 1 without any problems, the model with any EBPs (Model 2, χ^2 [1] = 5.23, $p < 0.05$) and the model with emotional or behavioural problems (Model 3, χ^2 [2] = 6.04, $p < 0.05$) showed a better fit in the likelihood ratio test and AIC. However, the BIC and AUCs were similar across models, which indicates that the incremental validity may not be substantial. In these models controlling for Level of Risk and other covariates, having any EBPs, having behavioural problems, or having conduct problems increased the odds of re-offending by 1.67 times (95% CI [1.08, 2.61]), 1.78 times (95% CI [1.12, 2.81]), and 2.05 times (95% CI [1.20, 3.50]), respectively.

6.5 Summary and Implications

This chapter examined a subsample of 545 young offenders under community supervision. Our aim was to assess the associations between YLS/CMI Level of Risk, EBPs, and re-offending rate. We also sought to determine the incremental validity of including the assessment of EBPs to Level of Risk for predicting 2-year re-offending after the start of the order. The findings and implications are summarised below.

6.5.1 YLS/CMI Level of Risk Is the Strongest Predictor of Re-offending

Our results are consistent with past research demonstrating that the Level of Risk from YLS/CMI 2.0 is a good predictor of re-offending. In our study, High-Risk young offenders had higher re-offending rates, compared to Moderate-Risk or Low-Risk youths. Additionally, High-Risk youths had more than 13 times the risk of re-offending compared to Low-Risk youth. The predictive accuracy of the Level of Risk was also supported, with an AUC of 0.71, which is at the higher end of the 0.51 to 0.78 found in a review of 11 studies (Schwalbe, 2007).

Importantly, Level of Risk remained the best predictor of re-offending even after including EBP variables. While EBPs increased the odds of re-offending by 1.67

Table 6.4 Results of logistic regression, AUC, fit indices, and model comparisons

	(1) Level of Risk only		(2) + Any EBPs		(3) + Emo/Beh problems		(4) + Specific problems	
	OR	95%CI	OR	95%CI	OR	95%CI	OR	95%CI
Chinese	0.48**	[0.30,0.76]	0.51**	[0.31,0.80]	0.50**	[0.31,0.80]	0.49**	[0.30,0.79]
Age	0.77***	[0.67,0.89]	0.77***	[0.67,0.89]	0.78***	[0.67,0.90]	0.78***	[0.67,0.90]
Female	0.92	[0.52,1.56]	0.95	[0.54,1.62]	0.96	[0.54,1.64]	0.95	[0.53,1.64]
YLS/CMI - Moderate-Risk	7.62**	[2.24,47.83]	7.47**	[2.18,46.97]	7.13**	[2.08,44.81]	7.30**	[2.12,46.03]
YLS/CMI - High-Risk	13.00***	[3.82,81.44]	10.88**	[3.16,68.53]	10.23**	[2.95,64.62]	10.23**	[2.91,65.06]
EBPs								
Any problem			1.67*	[1.08,2.61]				
Any emotional					0.88	[0.50,1.51]		
Depression							1.27	[0.65,2.41]
Anxiety problems							0.41	[0.13,1.115]
Somatic problems							1.60	[0.51,4.62]
Any behavioural					1.78*	[1.12,2.81]		
ADHD							0.99	[0.40,2.28]
Oppositional problems							0.71	[0.37,1.34]
Conduct problems							2.05**	[1.20,3.50]
Substance dependence							1.35	[0.68,2.59]
AUC	0.71		0.71		0.72		0.73	
AIC	551.26		548.04		549.22		553.18	
BIC	577.07		578.14		583.63		609.09	
Likelihood ratio χ^2 (df)	59.56 (5)***		64.79 (6)***		65.61 (7)***		71.64 (12)***	
ΔLikelihood ratio χ^2 model 1 (df)			5.23 (1)*		6.04 (2)*		12.08 (7)	

Note: Reference categories: race (Non-Chinese), sex (male), YLS/CMI Level of Risk (Low-Risk). Dependent variable is any re-offence within 2 years of index offence

$^{*}p < 0.05$, $^{**}p < 0.01$, $^{***}p < 0.001$

times, YLS/CMI Moderate-Risk and High-Risk increased the odds of re-offending by 7.47 times and 10.88 times, respectively, as compared to Low-Risk. These findings add to the current literature on the predictive validity of YLS/CMI in non-Western countries (Chu et al., 2015, 2020) and additionally show the comparative importance of YLS/CMI Level of Risk over EBPs in predicting re-offending.

The findings reinforced the validity of YLS/CMI but also revealed an area for improvement in the assessment tool. The YLS/CMI is effective in correctly identifying youths who do not re-offend (only 3.2% of youths classified as Low-Risk re-offended). However, there is room for improvement in its ability to identify youths who do re-offend (only 34.2% of youths classified as High-Risk re-offended). Other indicators, such as EBPs, have the potential to improve the YLS/CMI's effectiveness at identifying youths who are likely to re-offend.

6.5.2 Behavioural Problems Had Incremental Validity over YLS/CMI Level of Risk

We found that EBPs improved YLS/CMI's ability to predict re-offending in young offenders. Among youths of similar Levels of Risk, those with EBPs had higher re-offending rates. Moreover, EBPs had incremental validity over YLS/CMI Level of Risk in predicting re-offending. Including EBPs into the model showed a better fit to the data compared to the model using only Level of Risk. When looking at specific EBPs, behavioural problems, but not emotional problems, were a significant predictor of re-offending after controlling for Level of Risk. Overall, EBPs improves YLS/CMI's predictive ability, and this is mainly driven by behavioural rather than emotional problems.

Our results differ from past studies which showed that EBPs did not have any incremental validity (Guebert & Olver, 2014; McCormick et al., 2017). One reason could be that past studies excluded any overlapping EBPs and YLS/CMI criminogenic needs. For example, McCormick et al. (2017) excluded behavioural problems such as ADHD, conduct problems, oppositional defiant problems, and substance use problems because these problems were similar to the criminogenic factors of antisocial cognitions, antisocial personality pattern, and substance abuse. Yet it is precisely behavioural problems which had incremental validity over YLS/CMI in our study. Therefore, this study adds to the literature by showing that, even though behavioural problems overlap with YLS/CMI criminogenic needs, these two factors are different, and each can play a role in predicting re-offending. It is likely that behavioural problems encompass more diverse problems which are predictive of re-offending than the ones measured by the criminogenic needs.

Our results also highlight the importance of considering responsivity factors such as EBPs during assessment. However, studies on how correctional officers use risk assessment tools suggest that many officers focused on risk and needs factors, relegating responsivity factors to a minor role. In one study, correctional officers did not identify any responsivity factors in 80% of young offenders (Luong & Wormith, 2011). This could be due to correctional officers' perception that completing the YLS/CMI was a drain on their time in collecting all relevant information for assessment (Guy et al., 2014). Our findings suggest that correctional officers should not ignore responsivity factors in a complete assessment of youths' re-offending risk. Responsivity factors are important as they influence the effectiveness of rehabilitation programmes for the individual, which in turn impacts re-offending (Andrews et al., 2011).

One area for future research is on specific types of re-offending. While the present study examined general re-offending, previous studies found that EBPs had stronger associations with crimes such as arson and assaults rather than sexual and property crimes (Vinkers et al., 2011). Chapter 6 also shows that behavioural problems are associated with drug use. Additionally, depression was associated with violent crimes (Fazel et al., 2015) and antisocial personality disorder with extortion, robbery, and kidnapping (Pondé et al., 2014). Another area for research is the impact of sex differences on EBPs and re-offending. While sex was not a significant predictor of re-offending in our study, Wibbelink et al. (2017)'s systematic review showed that sex moderated the effect of emotional problems on re-offending, in that emotional problems were a *protective* factor for re-offending in females. No moderating effect was found for behavioural problems and re-offending. However, Wibbelink et al. (2017) acknowledged that studies on sex differences in EBPs and re-offending are lacking and thus need further research.

6.5.3 Screening for EBPs, Especially in High-Risk Young Offenders

Screening for EBPs is important as we found high rates of EBPs in young offenders. Rates of EBPs ranged from 20.8% in Low-Risk youths to 65.3% in High-Risk youths. Screening is especially important for High-Risk youths who are most likely to have EBPs. Additionally, screening should include emotional and behavioural problems, even though our findings showed that only behavioural problems predicted re-offending. All EBPs are potential barriers to treatment and should be treated alongside criminogenic needs (Jung & Dowker, 2016). For example, offenders with emotional problems such as anxiety may not respond well in group treatment (Andrews et al., 2011). Additionally, screening for EBPs would prevent underdiagnosis. As shown in Chap. 3, four in ten young offenders had self-reported problems but did not have a corresponding EBP diagnosis. Including a screening test allows case workers a more accurate assessment of the risk and needs of these young offenders and increases the success of interventions.

We recommend using brief EBP screening tools to prevent further strain on correctional officers' limited time (Guy et al., 2014). A review of EBP screening tools used in correctional settings identified some promising tools (Martin et al., 2013) such as the 8-item Brief Jail Mental Health Screen (Steadman et al., 2005), the 12-item Correctional Mental Health Screen for Men (Ford et al., 2007), the 8-item Correctional Mental Health Screen for Women (Ford et al., 2007), and the 4-item England Mental Health Screen (Grubin et al., 2002). Correctional agencies can use these EBP screening tools as a first step in addressing any EBPs in youths under their supervision.

Additionally, future research could explore how a brief EBP screening would work with a similarly simplified YLS/CMI risk measurement. Having a short and easy way to screen for EBPs and criminogenic needs would save time for correctional officers to focus on rehabilitation efforts. There are three simplified YLS/CMI instruments available in the literature. The 8-item YLS/CMI – Screening Version (YLS/CMI-SV) was developed by Hoge and Andrews (2009) with each item representing one of the eight criminogenic needs. Studies show good predictive validity for violent, non-violent, and general re-offending for the YLS/CMI-SV in young offenders (Chu et al., 2014). The 10-item YLS/CMI Brief Screener measured four out of the eight criminogenic needs (education/employment, peers, leisure, and personality) and was valid in predicting re-offending in both male and female young offenders (Campbell et al., 2014). Finally, the 7-item YLS/CMI Short Version measured five of the eight criminogenic needs (education/employment, peers, personality, attitudes, and family) with good predictive ability for similar youths from Spain, Portugal, and Canada (Basto-Pereira et al., 2021; Villanueva et al., 2020). However, more research is needed to examine how brief EBP screening tools could improve the predictive accuracy of these brief YLS/CMI measurements.

References

Andrews, D. A., Bonta, J., & Wormith, J. S. (2011). The risk-need-responsivity (RNR) model: Does adding the good lives model contribute to effective crime prevention? *Criminal Justice and Behavior, 38*(7), 735–755. https://doi.org/10.1177/0093854811406356

Australian Institute of Health and Welfare. (2018). *Young people returning to sentenced youth justice supervision 2016-17*. Australian Institute of Health and Welfare. https://www.aihw.gov.au/getmedia/48ae3545-83c5-46f1-96d4-9fac034fc71b/aihw-juv-127.pdf.aspx?inline=true

Baglivio, M. T., Wolff, K. T., Piquero, A. R., DeLisi, M., & Vaughn, M. G. (2017). Multiple pathways to juvenile recidivism: Examining parental drug and mental health problems, and markers of neuropsychological deficits among serious juvenile offenders. *Criminal Justice and Behavior, 44*(8), 1009–1029. https://doi.org/10.1177/0093854817714810

Basto-Pereira, M., & Farrington, D. P. (2022). Developmental predictors of offending and persistence in crime: A systematic review of meta-analyses. *Aggression and Violent Behavior, 65*, 101761. https://doi.org/10.1016/j.avb.2022.101761

Basto-Pereira, M., Villanueva, L., Peterson-Badali, M., Pimentel, A., Quintas, J., Cuervo, K., Hoge, R. D., & Skilling, T. A. (2021). Is a 7-item combination from the YLS/CMI an effective screening strategy for risk to reoffend? Findings from a cross-national study. *Criminal Justice and Behavior, 48*(5), 655–670. https://doi.org/10.1177/0093854821995866

Brooker, C., Sirdifield, C., & Marples, R. (2020). Mental health and probation: A systematic review of the literature. *Forensic Science International: Mind and Law, 1*, 100003. https://doi.org/10.1016/j.fsiml.2019.100003

Campbell, C., Onifade, E., Barnes, A., Peterson, J., Anderson, V., Davidson, W., & Gordon, D. (2014). Screening offenders: The exploration of a youth level of service/case management inventory (YLS/CMI) brief screener. *Journal of Offender Rehabilitation, 53*(1), 19–34. https://doi.org/10.1080/10509674.2013.861314

Chu, C. M., Yu, H., Lee, Y., & Zeng, G. (2014). The utility of the YLS/CMI-SV for assessing youth offenders in Singapore. *Criminal Justice and Behavior, 41*(12), 1437–1457. https://doi.org/10.1177/0093854814537626

Chu, C. M., Lee, Y., Zeng, G., Yim, G., Tan, C. Y., Ang, Y., Chin, S., & Ruby, K. (2015). Assessing youth offenders in a non-Western context: The predictive validity of the YLS/CMI ratings. *Psychological Assessment, 27*(3), 1013–1021. https://doi.org/10.1037/a0038670

Chu, C. M., Xu, X., Li, D., Ruby, K., & Chng, G. S. (2020). The utility of SAPROF-YV ratings for predicting recidivism in male youth under community supervision in Singapore. *Criminal Justice and Behavior, 47*(11), 1409–1427. https://doi.org/10.1177/0093854820949595

Chua, J. R., Chu, C. M., Yim, G., Chong, D., & Teoh, J. (2014). Implementation of the risk–need–responsivity framework across the juvenile justice agencies in Singapore. *Psychiatry, Psychology and Law, 21*(6), 877–889. https://doi.org/10.1080/13218719.2014.918076

Fazel, S., Wolf, A., Chang, Z., Larsson, H., Goodwin, G. M., & Lichtenstein, P. (2015). Depression and violence: A Swedish population study. *The Lancet Psychiatry, 2*(3), 224–232. https://doi.org/10.1016/S2215-0366(14)00128-X

Ford, J. D., Trestman, R. L., Wiesbrock, V., & Wanli, Z. (2007). Development and validation of a brief mental health screening instrument for newly incarcerated adults. *Assessment, 14*(3), 279–299. https://doi.org/10.1177/1073191107302944

Grubin, D., Carson, D., & Parsons, S. (2002). *Report on new prison reception health screening arrangements: The results of a pilot study in 10 prisons*. University of Newcastle.

Guebert, A. F., & Olver, M. E. (2014). An examination of criminogenic needs, mental health concerns, and recidivism in a sample of violent young offenders: Implications for risk, need, and responsivity. *International Journal of Forensic Mental Health, 13*(4), 295–310. https://doi.org/10.1080/14999013.2014.955220

Guy, L. S., Nelson, R. J., Fusco-Morin, S. L., & Vincent, G. M. (2014). What do juvenile probation officers think of using the SAVRY and YLS/CMI for case management, and do they use the instruments properly? *International Journal of Forensic Mental Health, 13*(3), 227–241. https://doi.org/10.1080/14999013.2014.939789

Hein, S., Barbot, B., Square, A., Chapman, J., Geib, C. F., & Grigorenko, E. L. (2017). Violent offending among juveniles: A 7-year longitudinal study of recidivism, desistance, and associations with mental health. *Law and Human Behavior, 41*(3), 273–283. https://doi.org/10.1037/lhb0000241

Hilterman, E. L. B., Nicholls, T. L., & van Nieuwenhuizen, C. (2014). Predictive validity of risk assessments in juvenile offenders: Comparing the SAVRY, PCL:YV, and YLS/CMI with unstructured clinical assessments. *Assessment, 21*(3), 324–339. https://doi.org/10.1177/1073191113498113

Hoeve, M., McReynolds, L. S., & Wasserman, G. A. (2013). The influence of adolescent psychiatric disorder on young adult recidivism. *Criminal Justice and Behavior, 40*(12), 1368–1382. https://doi.org/10.1177/0093854813488106

Hoge, R. D., & Andrews, D. A. (2009). *Youth level of service/case management inventory–Screening version*. Multi-Health Systems.

Hoge, R. D., & Andrews, D. A. (2011). *Youth level of service/case management inventory 2.0 (YLS/CMI 2.0): User's manual*. Multi-health systems.

Jung, S., & Dowker, B. A. (2016). Responsivity factors among offenders. *Journal of Offender Rehabilitation, 55*(3), 148–167. https://doi.org/10.1080/10509674.2016.1148090

Li, D., Chu, C. M., Xu, X., Zeng, G., & Ruby, K. (2019). Risk and protective factors for probation success among youth offenders in Singapore. *Youth Violence and Juvenile Justice, 17*(2), 194–213. https://doi.org/10.1177/1541204018778887

Luong, D., & Wormith, J. S. (2011). Applying risk/need assessment to probation practice and its impact on the recidivism of young offenders. *Criminal Justice and Behavior, 38*(12), 1177–1199. https://doi.org/10.1177/0093854811421596

Martin, M. S., Colman, I., Simpson, A. I. F., & McKenzie, K. (2013). Mental health screening tools in correctional institutions: A systematic review. *BMC Psychiatry, 13*(1), 275. https://doi.org/10.1186/1471-244X-13-275

McCarter, J. (2012). 2012 Annual report*: Office of the Auditor General of Ontario*. Queen's Printer for Ontario. https://www.auditor.on.ca/en/content/annualreports/arreports/en12/2012ar_en.pdf.

McCormick, S., Peterson-Badali, M., & Skilling, T. A. (2017). The role of mental health and specific responsivity in juvenile justice rehabilitation. *Law and Human Behavior, 41*(1), 55–67. https://doi.org/10.1037/lhb0000228

McReynolds, L. S., Schwalbe, C. S., & Wasserman, G. A. (2010). The contribution of psychiatric disorder to juvenile recidivism. *Criminal Justice and Behavior, 37*(2), 204–216. https://doi.org/10.1177/0093854809354961

Ministry of Justice. (2018a). *Proven re-offending tables (annual average), January 2017 to March 2017*. Ministry of Justice. https://assets.publishing.service.gov.uk/government/uploads/system/uploads/attachment_data/file/774865/proven-re-offending-jan17-mar17-annual.ods

Ministry of Justice. (2018b). *Youth justice indicators summary report April 2018*. Ministry of Justice. https://www.justice.govt.nz/assets/Youth-Justice-Indicators-Summary-Report-201804.pdf

Morgan, R. D., Scanlon, F., & Van Horn, S. A. (2020). Criminogenic risk and mental health: A complicated relationship. *CNS Spectrums, 25*(2), 237–244. https://doi.org/10.1017/s109285291900141x

Olver, M. E., Stockdale, K. C., & Wong, S. C. P. (2012). Short and long-term prediction of recidivism using the youth level of service/case management inventory in a sample of serious young offenders. *Law and Human Behavior, 36*(4), 331–344. https://doi.org/10.1037/h0093927

Onifade, E., Davidson, W., Campbell, C., Turke, G., Malinowski, J., & Turner, K. (2008). Predicting recidivism in probationers with the youth level of service case/ management inventory (YLS/CMI). *Criminal Justice and Behavior, 35*(4), 474–483. https://doi.org/10.1177/0093854807313427

Pondé, M. P., Caron, J., Mendonça, M. S. S., Freire, A. C. C., & Moreau, N. (2014). The relationship between mental disorders and types of crime in inmates in a Brazilian prison. *Journal of Forensic Sciences, 59*(5), 1307–1314. https://doi.org/10.1111/1556-4029.12462

Remschmidt, H., & Walter, R. (2010). The long-term outcome of delinquent children: A 30-year follow-up study. *Journal of Neural Transmission, 117*(5), 663–677. https://doi.org/10.1007/s00702-010-0393-8

Schwalbe, C. S. (2007). Risk assessment for juvenile justice: A meta-analysis. *Law and Human Behavior, 31*(5), 449–462. https://doi.org/10.1007/s10979-006-9071-7

Steadman, H. J., Scott, J. E., Osher, F., Agnese, T. K., & Robbins, P. C. (2005). Validation of the brief jail mental health screen. *Psychiatric Services, 56*(7), 816–822. https://doi.org/10.1176/appi.ps.56.7.816

Texas Juvenile Justice Department. (2018). *Annual report to the governor and legislative budget board 2018*. Texas Juvenile Justice Department. https://www.tjjd.texas.gov/index.php/doc-library/send/615-archive/1591-tjjd-annual-report-to-the-governor-and-legislative-budget-board-2018

Ting, M. H., Chu, C. M., Zeng, G., Li, D., & Chng, G. S. (2017). Predicting recidivism among youth offenders: Augmenting professional judgement with machine learning algorithms. *Journal of Social Work, 18*(6), 631–649. https://doi.org/10.1177/1468017317743137

Tsagris, M., & Pandis, N. (2021). Multicollinearity. *American Journal of Orthodontics and Dentofacial Orthopedics, 159*(5), 695–696. https://doi.org/10.1016/j.ajodo.2021.02.005

Villanueva, L., Basto-Pereira, M., & Cuervo, K. (2020). How to improve the YLS/CMI? Exploring a particularly predictive combination of items. *International Journal of Offender Therapy and Comparative Criminology, 64*(9), 922–937. https://doi.org/10.1177/0306624x19881926

Vinkers, D. J., de Beurs, E., Barendregt, M., Rinne, T., & Hoek, H. W. (2011). The relationship between mental disorders and different types of crime. *Criminal Behaviour and Mental Health, 21*(5), 307–320. https://doi.org/10.1002/cbm.819

Wei, Z., Homel, R., Prichad, J., & Xu, J. (2004). Patterns of juvenile offending in Shanghai and Brisbane. *The Australian and New Zealand Journal of Criminology, 37*(1), 32–51. https://doi.org/10.1177/00048658040370S103

Wibbelink, C. J. M., Hoeve, M., Stams, G. J. J. M., & Oort, F. J. (2017). A meta-analysis of the association between mental disorders and juvenile recidivism. *Aggression and Violent Behavior, 33*, 78–90. https://doi.org/10.1016/j.avb.2017.01.005

Willner, C. J., Gatzke-Kopp, L. M., & Bray, B. C. (2016). The dynamics of internalizing and externalizing comorbidity across the early school years. *Development and Psychopathology, 28*(4), 1033–1052. https://doi.org/10.1017/s0954579416000687

Xu, X., Li, D., Chu, C. M., Chng, G. S., & Ruby, K. (2020). Understanding changes in youth offenders' risk profiles: A latent transition analysis. *Youth Violence and Juvenile Justice, 18*(3), 294–312. https://doi.org/10.1177/1541204019883922

Yukhnenko, D., Blackwood, N., & Fazel, S. (2020). Risk factors for recidivism in individuals receiving community sentences: A systematic review and meta-analysis. *CNS Spectrums, 25*(2), 252–263. https://doi.org/10.1017/s1092852919001056

Chapter 7
Protective Factors Against Emotional and Behavioural Problems in Young Offenders

Mengru Liu, Dennis Teo, and Chi Meng Chu

Contents

Youths face several potential stressors (e.g., physical conditions, academic problems, as well as peer pressure) in their daily lives (World Health Organization, 2021). If these stressors are not well managed, they can affect the youths' daily functioning and quality of life; ultimately leading, possibly, to the development of mental health disorders (Thoits, 2013).

However, stressors may not always lead to problematic outcomes. Youths may show resilience when they encounter stressors if they draw on sufficient protective factors (Rutter, 1987; Masten, 2001). Protective factors could buffer youths against adversity and reduce the negative effects of stressors, thus resulting in a lower likelihood of problematic outcomes (O'Connell et al., 2009). These protective factors can

M. Liu (✉) · D. Teo
National Council of Social Service, Singapore, Singapore
e-mail: liu_mengru@ncss.gov.sg

C. M. Chu
Ministry of Social and Family Development, National Council of Social Service, Singapore, Singapore

D. Li et al. (eds.), *Emotional and Behavioural Problems of Young Offenders in Singapore*, SpringerBriefs in Criminology,
https://doi.org/10.1007/978-3-031-41702-3_7

Table 7.1 Unstandardised parameter estimates and variances of intercept and slope of the fitted LGCMs

	Intercept (I)		Slope (S)	
	Estimates	Variances	Estimates	Variances
EBPs				
Emotional problems	58.33**	2.15**	−2.82**	0.21**
Behavioural problems	63.46**	3.20**	−4.10**	0.49**
External factors				
Family functioning	2.08**	0.04*	0.06**	0.05**
Parent attachment	3.56**	0.41**	0.07**	0.06**
Home assets	2.91**	0.22**	0.06*	0.03**
Peer assets	3.16**	0.16**	0.03	0.06**
School assets	2.87**	0.16**	−0.02	0.02*
Community assets	2.69**	0.27**	0.05**	0.08**
Internal factors				
Cooperation and communication	2.98**	0.18**	0.02	0.02*
Empathy	3.18**	0.21**	0.03*	0.04**
Goal and aspiration	3.28**	0.23**	−0.05**	0.05**
Problem-solving	2.83**	0.27**	0.05**	0.06**
Self-efficacy	2.92**	0.16**	0.05**	0.03**
Self-awareness	3.04**	0.26**	0.04*	0.06**

Note: *LGCM* latent growth curve model
$*p < 0.05$, $**p < 0.01$

be categorised into external or internal assets according to the developmental assets framework (Leffert et al., 1998). External assets refer to health-promoting factors in social settings, whereas internal assets refer to personal attributes (e.g., values, characteristics, and competencies; Leffert et al., 1998). Youths with the most total external and internal assets were found to be the least likely to engage in negative behaviours such as suicidal attempts, violence, and substance use (Leffert et al., 1998; Kingon & O'Sullivan, 2001).

Several protective factors for good youth mental health development have been found in prior studies. Externally, social and family support, neighbourhood and community engagement (Triana et al., 2019, O'Connell et al., 2009), robust social networks and connections (Son et al., 2020), acceptance by parents and peers (Steinhausen & Metzke, 2001), and free psychological help in community (Sharma et al., 2020) were all found to be effective protective factors. For internal factors, high self-esteem (Steinhausen & Metzke, 2001; Triana et al., 2019), self-compassion (Tanaka et al., 2011), emotional self-regulation, good coping skills (Sharma et al., 2020), and problem-solving skills (O'Connell et al., 2009) were found to be important for youth mental health, including young offenders (Li et al., 2021).

Though the research around protective factors is an active industry, few studies have investigated the longitudinal associations between protective factors and emotional and behavioural problems (EBPs). This chapter aims to identify protective factors of various mental health conditions in young offenders as they are particularly vulnerable to EBPs (Rijo et al., 2016). We considered a list of potential protective factors based on past research and examined how these factors changed alongside the EBPs of young offenders over time. Factors that were closely associated with changes in EBPs were more likely to be effective protective factors. Potential protective factors investigated in this chapter include external factors that stem from social relationships and internal factors that stem from an individual's personal competence. Similar to previous chapters, we explored mental health conditions along two broad dimensions: emotional and behavioural problems. The severity of these EBPs, rather than the presence, is examined in this chapter. By understanding the factors that help youths stay resilient in the face of mental health challenges, the findings in this chapter can aid the development of effective prevention strategies for addressing mental health issues.

7.1 Changes in EBPs, External, and Internal Protective Factors

Before we examined how EBPs and potential protective factors change together over time, we first estimated the individual trajectories of each EBP and potential protective factor over time. We performed latent growth curve modelling (on each variable separately) to estimate these growth trajectories using the longitudinal sample of 835 young offenders. The offenders' demographics, including their age, sex, and race, were controlled in each model. Intercept factors and slope factors were estimated to represent the trajectories of each variable (e.g., behavioural problems). The intercept factors represent the initial status when the youths first entered the justice system (baseline at Wave 1), and the slope factors represent the linear rates of change from Wave 1 to Wave 3. The latent growth curve models fitted the data well. The intercept and slope factors used to model the trajectories of EBPs, as well as the potential protective factors, are reported in Table 7.1.

7.1.1 EBP Trajectories

As described in Chap. 2, we used the YSR/ASR to measure emotional and behavioural problems. Emotional problems refer to emotional distress within the self, whereas behavioural problems refer to problematic behaviours towards others in the external world (Achenbach, 1991; Bongers et al., 2003). Measures of emotional problems include 29 items, such as "I worry a lot", and measures of behavioural problems include 27 items, such as "I disobey at school". Respondents reported how applicable the items were to reflect their conditions of the previous 6 months by rating on three-point scales, from *not true (0)* and *somewhat or sometimes true (1) to very true or often true (2)*. Their raw scores were further converted to T-scores. Higher scores indicate that the respondent is facing more problems. A T-score of 60 is the borderline clinical score, and a T-score of 64 and above is an indicator of having emotional or behavioural problems within the clinical range (Achenbach, 1991).

Consistent with changes in EBPs, which were reported in Chaps. 4 and 5, we found similar decreasing trends for emotional as well as behavioural problems in our sample of youths who had offended. At baseline, the average T-score of our participants' emotional problems was 58.34, whereas the average T-score of behavioural problems was 63.46. Considering the cut-off scores for being in the borderline clinical (≥ 60) or the clinical range (≥ 64), our sample started with having emotional problems close to the borderline and behavioural problems close to the clinical range. Over time, the youths' emotional problems decreased significantly by −2.82 each year on average ($p < 0.01$), and their behavioural problems decreased significantly by −4.01 each year ($p < 0.01$), on average. These trends are encouraging as they show that young offenders experienced less EBPs over time after entering the justice system. For the sake of illustration, consider that the average youth has a T-score of 63.46 in behavioural problems at baseline. After 1 year, the average youth's behavioural T-score falls within the normal range (59.45) and continues to improve to healthier levels in the subsequent year (55.44). That said, the levels of emotional and behavioural problems that plague these young offenders are still much higher than the general population. The LONGSCAN study investigated a sample of 825 non-offender youths in the USA and found an average T-score of 50.0 for emotional problems and 50.1 for behavioural problems (Knight & O'Sullivan, 2001), substantially lower than the current sample. Hence, it is still important to identify effective protective factors that could further alleviate the EBPs of young offenders.

7.1.2 External and Internal Protective Factors' Trajectories

We identified a set of potential external protective factors arising from social relationships across multiple contextual settings, such as family, peer, school, and community. We also identified potential internal protective factors which consist of six facets of personal competence: cooperation and communication, empathy, goal and aspiration, problem-solving, self-efficacy, and self-awareness.

Family-related factors constitute general family functioning, parent attachment, and assets from the home environment. Family functioning refers to the overall quality of interactions amongst family members (Epstein et al., 1978; Minuchin et al., 2009). This construct was measured by 12 items (e.g., "We can express feelings to each other.") from The McMaster Family Assessment Device (FAD; Epstein et al., 1978). The youths rated all items on four-point scales ranging from *strongly agree* (1) to *strongly disagree* (4). The scores were reverse coded so higher scores indicate healthier family functioning. Parent attachment, which refers to the youth's perceptions of their overall attachment with their parents, was assessed by 25 items (e.g., "My mother respects my feelings.") from the revised Inventory of Parent and Peer Attachment (IPPA). Scores ranged from 1 (*almost never or never true*) to 5 (*almost always or always true*). Higher scores imply higher parental attachment (Armsden & Greenberg, 1987). Home assets indicate caring and supportive connections, high expectations, and meaningful participation amongst families (Constantine & Benard, 2001).

The other external assets (outside the family context) that we studied include assets from peers, school, and community. Similar to home assets, they indicate the extent of high-quality connections, expectations, and interactions that the youth has within each social context. These assets were measured by the Resilience and Youth Development Module (RYDM); see a summary of items for each construct in Chap. 2. A four-point scale ranging from *not at all true* (1) to *very much true* (4) was adopted for each item. Higher scores imply that the respondent has more protective assets.

For internal factors, we investigated assets that arise from the youth's personal competence which include cooperation and communication, empathy, goal and aspiration, problem-solving, self-efficacy, and self-awareness. These internal assets refer to individual qualities, strengths, and characteristics linked with desirable developmental outcomes (Constantine & Benard, 2001). Cooperation and communication refers to social competence; empathy refers to understanding and caring about another's feelings; goals and aspirations refers to having dreams, visions, and plans towards the future; problem-solving refers to the ability to plan and think thoroughly before making a decision or taking action; and self-efficacy refers to the belief in one's ability to do something, whereas self-awareness refers to knowing and understanding one's self (Constantine & Benard, 2001). Similar to the external assets, these internal assets were measured by the RYDM. Higher scores imply that the respondent has more protective assets.

Overall, our results revealed that almost all of these factors, both internal and external, improved over time on average. This improving trend can be observed from the negative slopes of EBPs and the positive slopes of protective factors (see Table 7.1). These overall desirable changes in mental health, social relationships, and personal competence of young offenders are encouraging from a rehabilitative perspective. The justice system aims to provide treatment for these youths so that they will have healthy outcomes, such as the successful reintegration into society, when they exit the justice system (Steinberg et al., 2004). Such treatments improve the psychosocial development of young offenders which translates into positive outcomes (Steinberg et al., 2004). Singapore, in particular, offers many rehabilitation programmes for young offenders to address the offenders' criminogenic thinking and behaviour, improve their prosocial skills, and incorporate maximum participation of their families and the community (Kamal, 2006).

Despite these overall positive trends, we found significant variations in the change patterns, implying that individuals differed in their rates of change (Farrington et al., 1988; Steinberg et al., 2004). Furthermore, the average improvements in peer assets, school assets, and cooperation and communication amongst young offenders were not significant. A likely explanation is that some social interactions of these youths are placed under restrictions and scrutiny within the justice system. They might not have been able to socially adapt to these changes, which suggests that there might be a need to implement programmes to orientate their social skills or facilitate their social interactions. We also found that their average goals and aspirations decreased after entering the justice system. Arguably, entering the justice system could affect the orientation towards their future for some youth (Steinberg et al., 2004). Offence charges, sanctions, and early criminal labelling may take away the eligibility of various careers for these young offenders (Oyserman & Markus, 1990; Moffitt, 2017). Thus, their views of their "possible selves" and aspirations towards the future might be impaired, which explains the decreasing goals and aspirations found in our study. In the next section, we will further explore the effects of protective factors whilst accounting for the different change patterns.

7.2 Identifying Effective Protective Factors

As mentioned earlier, our main strategy to identify effective protective factors involves covarying the trajectories of the factors with the trajectories of emotional and behavioural problems. Assuming that an asset (e.g., home assets) is indeed a protective factor that guards young offenders from mental distress, we should see these variables covarying closely with one another across time. If a youth experiences an improvement in the asset, this should increase their resilience against mental health distress, leading to less emotional and/or behavioural problems. Conversely, if a youth experiences a decrease in the asset, we should expect them to be less able to cope with mental health difficulties and experience more emotional and/or behavioural problems. Corresponding changes will indicate that intervening and improving the identified protective factors can help reduce EBPs.

Since we have already estimated the individual trajectories of each variable (represented by their respective intercepts and slopes), we further conducted fully multivariate latent growth curve models to assess which factors' trajectories significantly predict the intercept and slope of EBPs. In the model, we simultaneously estimated a trajectory for the protective factor and EBPs to represent their changes over time. The standardised coefficients representing the associations between the trajectories of each factor and the youths' EBPs are summarised in Table 7.2. "I(A) to I(B)" represents the association between the two variables at baseline. "I(A) to S(B)" can be interpreted as the relationship between the factor at baseline and the changes in EBPs over time. This chapter is especially interested in the last coefficient, "S(A) to S(B)", which is the relationship between the slopes of the two variables. This reflects how changes in the factor affect changes in EBPs, which is useful for identifying effective protective factors. This yields good evidence of causal effects, since a key requirement for causality is that changes in the cause predict changes in its effect. Importantly, our analyses also study the within-individual changes in protective factors and EBPs (as opposed to between-individual changes). This accounts for many extraneous variables that would confound our causal interpretations. Three controlling variables, indexing the participants' age, sex, and race, were added to the

Table 7.2 Standardised coefficients of the fitted multivariate LGCMs

	EBPs (B)					
	Emotional problems			Behavioural problems		
Protective factors (A)	I(A) to I(B)	I(A) to S(B)	S(A) to S(B)	I(A) to I(B)	I(A) to S(B)	S(A) to S(B)
External-family						
Family functioning	−0.37**	−0.22*	−0.45**	−0.40**	−0.11	−0.42**
Parent attachment	−0.32**	−0.21**	−0.43**	−0.37**	−0.04	−0.41**
Attachment to mother	−0.29**	−0.19*	−0.38**	−0.34**	−0.07	−0.35**
Attachment to father	−0.23**	−0.25**	−0.40**	−0.27**	−0.10	−0.40**
Home assets	−0.10*	−0.27**	−0.33**	−0.12*	−0.17*	−0.34**
External-other						
Peer assets	−0.12	−0.09	−0.16	−0.25**	−0.16	−0.27
School assets	−0.03	−0.10	−0.20	−0.01	−0.10	0.06
Community assets	−0.02	−0.02	0.07	0.04	0.06	0.12
Internal-personal competence						
Cooperation and communication	−0.18**	−0.15	−0.37**	−0.26**	−0.02	−0.29*
Self-efficacy	−0.20**	−0.10	−0.38**	−0.07	−0.10	−0.20*
Empathy	0.14*	−0.17*	0.04	−0.17**	−0.01	0.05
Goal and aspiration	0.15**	−0.19**	−0.01	−0.03	−0.05	0.09
Problem-solving	−0.14*	−0.12	−0.22*	−0.12*	−0.06	−0.04
Self-awareness	−0.25**	−0.09	−0.34*	−0.22**	−0.04	−0.11

Note: *LGCM* latent growth curve model; *I* intercept; *S* slope
*$p < 0.05$, **$p < 0.01$

models. In the remainder of this section, we highlight our key findings from this analysis and discuss the effectiveness of the studied factors.

7.2.1 External Protective Factors: Family Context

A person's psychological well-being develops through interactions with other people in their proximal environments (Zhang et al., 2011). The family, being the most direct and recent microenvironment for youths, is pivotal to the development of their psychological well-being (Zeleke, 2013). Various constructs related to family have been consistently found to protect youths from mental health problems, including family functioning (Yang et al., 2014; Milburn et al., 2019), family support (Seidman et al., 1999; Symister & Friend, 2003), family cohesion (Van Dijk et al., 2014; Jhang, 2017), positive family communication (Carbonell et al., 1998; Thoits, 2013), and parenting involvement in schools (Richman et al., 1998). The findings all point to the family being a crucial influence on healthy youth development. Families care for each other, help each other, provide advice, and regulate each other's behaviours (Cohen, 2004; Reczek et al., 2014; Jhang, 2017). Good relationships and support amongst family members contribute to (a) the development of better interpersonal skills, self confidence, and greater sense of purpose, (b) the feeling of love and acceptance, as well as (c) better coping of stress and depression (e.g., Demir et al., 2011; Graziano et al., 2009; Wang et al., 2014).

Consistent with this, we found that family-related variables provide stable and strong buffering effects against EBPs. Results showed that at baseline, youths who had better family functioning, higher parent attachment, and better home assets had less EBPs. Youths with better baseline family assets were also more likely to experience stronger improvement in emotional problems (but not behavioural problems) over time.

Of special interest, we found that changes in family functioning, parent attachment, and home assets all had significant and positive effects on changes in emotional and behavioural problems. Improving these three family-related factors corresponded with more decrease in EBPs over time. To get an intuitive understanding of these effects, we compared the EBPs of youths experiencing three different trends of family-related protective factors over time: (1) youths who had above average change (+1 SD above average), (2) average change, and (3) below average change (−1 SD below average) in family-related factors. We can visualise how these three groups differentially change in EBPs over time in Figs. 7.1, 7.2, and 7.3 (one figure for each of the family-related factors). When there is an average improvement in family-related factors, there is typically a moderate decrease in EBPs over time. For those with above average improvement in these family-related factors, we observe a sharper decrease in EBPs over time. Finally, with below average improvement in family-related factors, we tend to see a maintained or moderately increased EBPs over time.

We can quantify these effects by comparing the EBPs of youths who experienced high improvement in family-related factors (+1 SD above the average change) against the youths with average change. Firstly, for family functioning, the youths

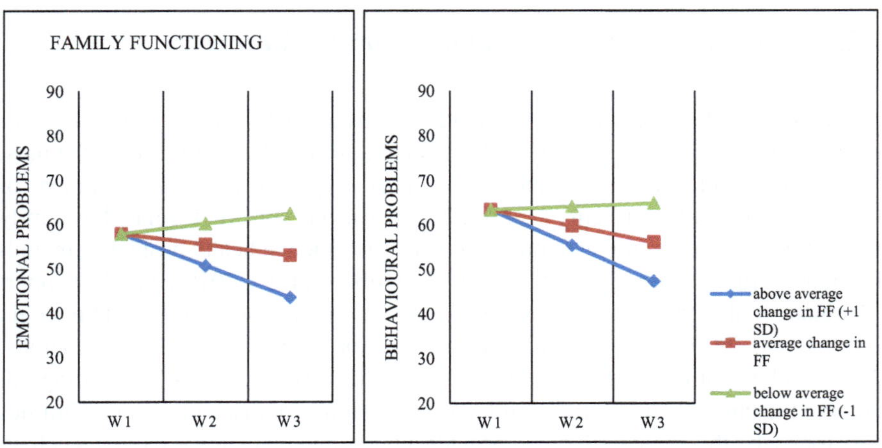

Fig. 7.1 Model estimates of EBPs at three levels of change in family functioning (FF) across waves (W)

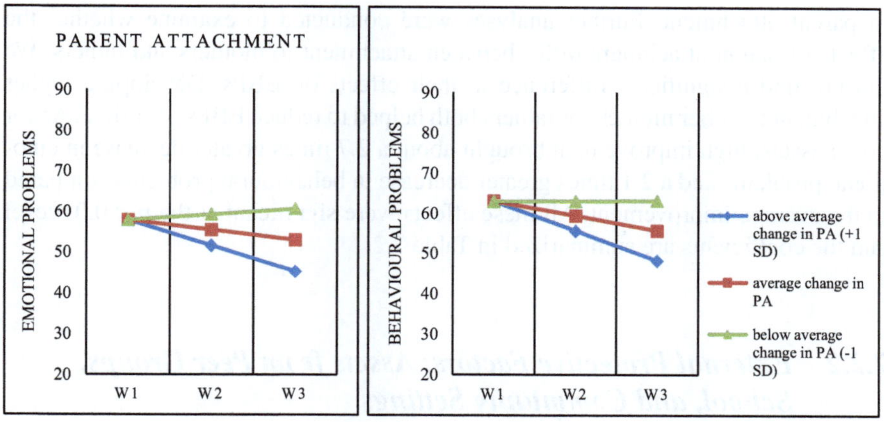

Fig. 7.2 Model estimates of EBPs at three levels of change in parent attachment (PA) across waves (W)

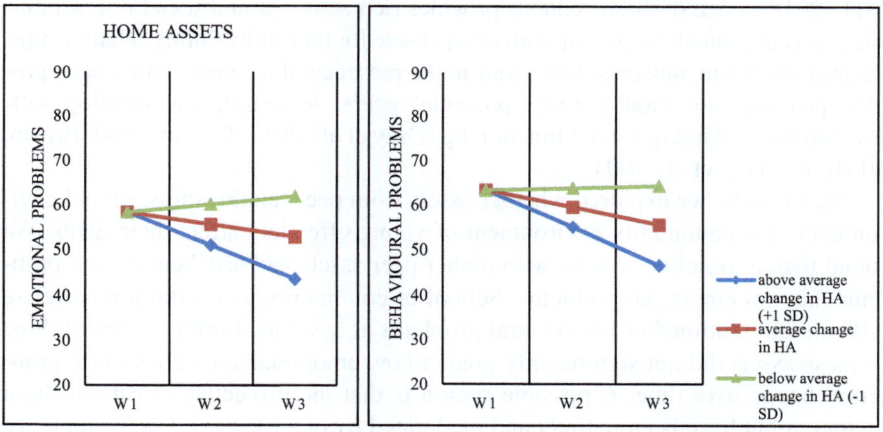

Fig. 7.3 Model estimates of EBPs at three levels of change in home assets (HA) across waves (W)

with average change experienced an average decrease of −2.42 per year in their T-score of emotional problems and an average decrease of −3.66 per year in behavioural problems. In contrast, youths with high improvement in family functioning (represented by the above average change group) experienced roughly a three times sharper decrease (−7.26 per year) in emotional problems and a 2.2 times sharper decrease (−8.05 per year) in behavioural problems over time compared to the youths with average change in family functioning. Moving onto the other family-related factors, youths who had high improvement in parent attachment experienced a 2.6 times greater decrease in emotional problems and a two times greater decrease in behavioural problems over time compared to youths with an average improvement in parent attachment. Further analyses were conducted to examine whether the effects of parent attachment differ between attachment to mothers and fathers. We did not find a significant difference in their effects on EBPs. Developing higher attachment to either mothers or fathers both helped to reduce EBPs over time. As for home assets, high improvement brought about a 2.7 times greater decrease in emotional problems and a 2.1 times greater decrease in behavioural problems compared to the average improvement. All these effects were significant at the $p < 0.01$ level and the coefficients are summarized in Table 7.2.

7.2.2 External Protective Factors: Assets from Peer Groups, School, and Community Settings

Outside of the family setting, other social contexts like peer groups, school, and community settings may also aid youths in their prosocial development (Graber et al., 2018). Each of these contexts provides rich activities and social interactions. They may accentuate social support, compensate for unhealthy family relationships, deter youths from antisocial behaviour in the presence of normative pressures, provide positive role models (e.g., prosocial peers, teachers), and develop self-competence and interpersonal functioning (Dray et al., 2017; Larson, 2000; Brown, 2004; Steinberg et al., 2004).

Accordingly, we explored whether assets from peer relationships, school environment, and community environment of young offenders affect their EBPs. We found that, at baseline, youths with higher peer assets had less behavioural problems, but not emotional problems. School or community assets did not correlate with either emotional or behavioural problems at baseline. Furthermore, all three of these assets did not significantly predict how emotional and behavioural problems change over time. A possible reason is that the protective effects of these factors might have been indirect and moderated by other factors. For example, Li et al. (2021) found buffering effects from peer assets and school/work assets against certain types of adversities, such as physical, emotional, or sexual abuse. Future work can test if these buffering effects interact with the type of adversities faced by the youths or other risk factors. Whilst there is still merit in exploring the potential protective effects of peer relationships, school environment, and community environment, our findings further highlight the importance of the family setting, which had a more direct and stable effect over time on the mental health of young offenders. This also echoes the finding in Chap. 4, where family assets were identified as the most prominent protective factor against depression. These converging results make a strong call for intervention programmes to target the family unit in their efforts to safeguard the external environments of young offenders.

7.2.3 Internal Protective Factors: Personal Competence

For internal factors, we investigated the effectiveness of six facets of personal competence: cooperation and communication, empathy, goal and aspiration, problem-solving, self-efficacy, and self-awareness as protective factors. There is a wealth of recent studies showing that these factors promote resilience and reduce mental health problems in youths (Dray et al., 2017, Beyond Blue, 2018; Masten, 2021). Here, we assessed the extent in which these factors covary with EBPs across time on our longitudinal sample of young offenders.

Results showed that cooperation and communication and self-efficacy were the most significant protective factors associated with decreased EBPs. At baseline, youths with higher cooperation and communication experienced less emotional and behavioural problems. Youths with higher self-efficacy had less emotional but not behavioural problems at baseline. Of interest, a higher increase in cooperation and communication and self-efficacy also significantly predicted a sharper decrease in EBPs over time. As before, we can compare youths with high improvement (above average change) in these internal assets against youths with average improvement to quantify the protective effects of these internal assets. Youths who had high improvement in cooperation and communication over time tended to experience a sharper decrease, roughly a 3.1 times greater decrease in emotional problems and a 2.1 times greater decrease in behavioural problems over time compared to youths who had an average change in cooperation and communication. Youths who had high improvement in self-efficacy over time also tended to experience roughly a three times greater decrease in emotional problems and a 1.7 times greater decrease in behavioural problems compared to youths with average improvement. The coefficients are summarized in Table 7.2, and these effects can be visualised in Figs. 7.4 and 7.5. The figures visually show that youths with above average change in

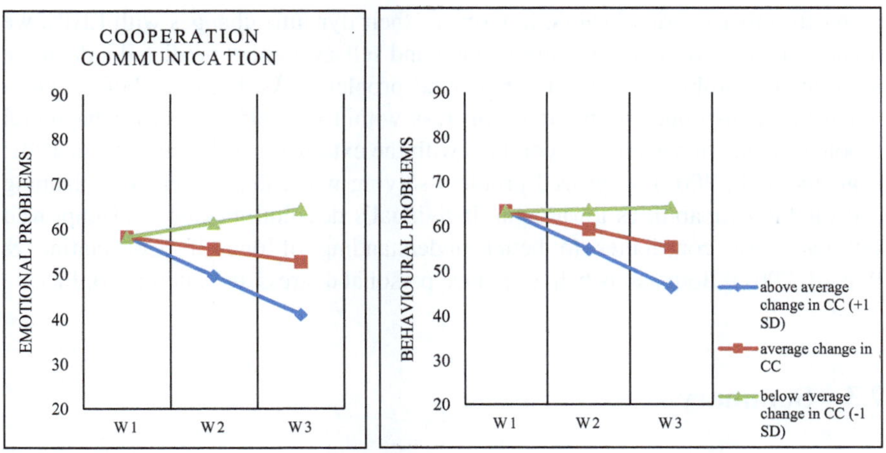

Fig. 7.4 Model estimates of EBPs at three levels of change in cooperation and communication (CC) across waves (W)

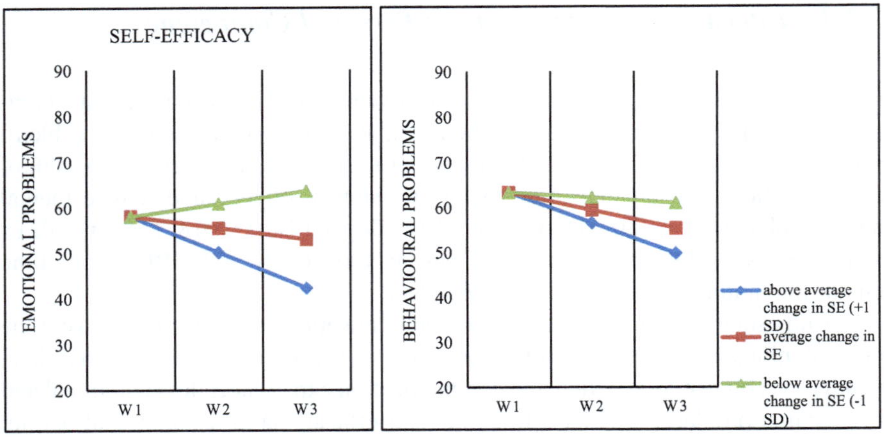

Fig. 7.5 Model estimates of EBPs at three levels of change in self-efficacy (SE) across waves (W)

cooperation and communication, and self-efficacy experienced the most decrease in EBPs over time (represented by the blue line with a diamond in Figs. 7.4 and 7.5) compared with youths with average or below average change.

Good cooperation and communication indicate higher social competence and prosocial skills, which promote interpersonal functioning. Well-functioning social interactions can guard against mental health distress and related mental illnesses (Dray et al., 2017). Meanwhile, increased self-efficacy involves higher self-esteem and more positive views of oneself (Fukukawa et al., 2000). Self-esteem, in turn, is an important psychological resource that people draw on to maintain optimism and increase positive affect, making it an effective buffer against mental health distress (Symister & Friend, 2003).

As for other internal factors, in terms of their dynamic changes with EBPs, we found that an increase in problem-solving and self-awareness predicted a decrease in emotional problems, but not behavioural problems. As discussed before, emotional problems concern emotional distress within the self, whereas behavioural problems concern behavioural conflicts with the external world (Achenbach, 1991; Bongers et al., 2003). Improved problem-solving will enhance personal planning and thinking capabilities towards an individual's decision-making, and improved self-awareness contributes to better understanding of oneself (Constantine & Benard, 2001). Both assets help to reduce personal distress and internal conflict.

7.3 Summary

This chapter showed that in young offenders, improvement in family functioning, parent attachment, home assets, cooperation and communication, and self-efficacy all grant protection against EBPs in the long run. Better self-awareness and problem-solving help these youths bounce back from emotional problems but not behavioural problems. Peer assets, school assets and community assets, goals and aspirations, and empathy were not found to have direct protective effects against EBPs amongst these youths. These findings refine our understanding of how internal and external protective factors relate to EBPs in young offenders.

Young offenders and non-offending youth have different treatment needs, especially so across different cultural contexts (Lai et al., 2016; Koh, et al., 2021). Identifying effective protective factors specific to these youths in Singapore can inform correctional agencies on precise areas for focused intervention (Hoge & Andrews, 2010). As a collectivist society, Singapore values family and family obligations, making family support an especially important factor to maintain mental health compared to individualistic cultures (Berkman et al., 2000; Koh, et al., 2021). Past research in Singapore also found Functional Family Therapy (FFT) to be effective for young offenders. Individuals who received FFT reported higher levels of well-being immediately and up to the end of their probation periods compared with those who did not (Gan et al., 2021). In line with this discussion, our findings show the dynamic relationship between family-related factors and EBPs. Youths who improved more in family-related factors tended to also decrease more in EBPs over time. These results theoretically support the need to implement family-based intervention on a larger scale and increase parental involvement in intervention programmes for young offenders. Such interventions could work on various facets of the family, including increasing understanding, supportiveness, openness, acceptance, belongingness, and meaningful activities within the family context.

Internally, the findings highlighted the need to include personal capabilities into treatment planning. Current cognitive interventions in Singapore include problem-solving, conflict resolution, responsible thinking, and self-control (Kamal, 2006; Koh et al., 2021; Ministry of Social and Family Development, 2022). Our findings recommend incorporating more physical activities, mindful processes, counselling, and therapy sessions (e.g., CBT) to improve individuals' self-efficacy and self-awareness (Williams & French, 2011). Apart from self-efficacy, we also identified cooperation and communication as a strong protective factor. Yet, it is also one of the few protective factors that remained unchanged, on average, in youths within the justice system. This signals a strong need to provide training for young offenders in areas such as enhancing their interpersonal skills (e.g., Lipsey, 2000). In sum, this chapter meaningfully adds to the evidence base for resilience-focused interventions which build supportive social structures or personal improvement programmes for youth.

References

Achenbach, T. M. (1991). *Manual for the youth self-report and 1991 profile*. Department of Psychiatry, University of Vermont.

Armsden, G. C., & Greenberg, M. T. (1987). The inventory of parent and peer attachment: Individual differences and their relationship to psychological well-being in adolescence. *Journal of youth and adolescence, 16*(5), 427–454.

Berkman, L. F., Glass, T., Brissette, I., & Seeman, T. E. (2000). From social integration to health: Durkheim in the new millennium. *Social Science & Medicine (1982), 51*(6), 843–857. https://doi.org/10.1016/s0277-9536(00)00065-4

Blue, B. (2018). *Building resilience in children aged 0–12-A practice guide*. Beyond Blue, 2017.

Bongers, I. L., Koot, H. M., van der Ende, J., & Verhulst, F. C. (2003). The normative development of child and adolescent problem behavior. *Journal of Abnormal Psychology, 112*(2), 179–192. https://doi.org/10.1037/0021-843x.112.2.179

Brown, B. B. (2004). Adolescents' relationships with peers. *Handbook of adolescent psychology*, 363–394. https://doi.org/10.1002/9780471726746.ch12

Carbonell, D. M., Reinherz, H. Z., & Giaconia, R. M. (1998). Risk and resilience in late adolescence. *Child and Adolescent Social Work Journal, 15*, 251–272. https://doi.org/10.1023/A:1025107827111

Cohen, S. (2004). Social relationships and health. *American psychologist, 59*(8), 676. https://doi.org/10.1037/0003-066X.59.8.676

Constantine, N. A., & Benard, B. (2001). California healthy kids survey resilience assessment module: Technical report. *Journal of Adolescent Health, 28*(2), 122–140.

Demir, T., Karacetin, G., Demir, D. E., & Uysal, O. (2011). Epidemiology of depression in an urban population of Turkish children and adolescents. *Journal of Affective Disorders, 134*(1–3), 168–176. https://doi.org/10.1016/j.jad.2011.05.041

Dray, J., Bowman, J., Campbell, E., Freund, M., Wolfenden, L., Hodder, R. K., McElwaine, K., Tremain, D., Bartlem, K., Bailey, J., Small, T., Palazzi, K., Oldmeadow, C., & Wiggers, J. (2017). Systematic review of universal resilience-focused interventions targeting child and adolescent mental health in the school setting. *Journal of the American Academy of Child & Adolescent Psychiatry, 56*(10), 813–824. https://doi.org/10.1016/j.jaac.2017.07.780

Epstein, N. B., Bishop, D. S., & Levin, S. (1978). The McMaster model of family functioning. *Journal of Marital and Family therapy, 4*(4), 19–31. https://doi.org/10.1111/j.1752-0606.1978.tb00537.x

Farrington, D. P., Gallagher, B., Morley, L., St Ledger, R. J., & West, D. J. (1988). Are there any successful men from criminogenic backgrounds? *Psychiatry, 51*(2), 116–130.

Fukukawa, Y., Tsuboi, S., Niino, N., Ando, F., Kosugi, S., & Shimokata, H. (2000). Effects of social support and self-esteem on depressive symptoms in Japanese middle-aged and elderly people. *Journal of epidemiology, 10*(1sup), 63–69. https://doi.org/10.2188/jea.10.1sup_63

Gan, D. Z., Zhou, Y., Abdul Wahab, N. D. B., Ruby, K., & Hoo, E. (2021). Effectiveness of functional family therapy in a non-western context: Findings from a randomized-controlled evaluation of youth offenders in Singapore. *Family Process, 60*(4), 1170–1184. https://doi.org/10.1111/famp.12630

Graber, J. A., Brooks-Gunn, J., & Petersen, A. C. (Eds.). (2018). *Transitions through adolescence: Interpersonal domains and context*. Psychology Press.

Graziano, F., Bonino, S., & Cattelino, E. (2009). Links between maternal and paternal support, depressive feelings and social and academic self-efficacy in adolescence. *European Journal of Developmental Psychology, 6*(2), 241–257. https://doi.org/10.1080/17405620701252066

Hoge, R. D., & Andrews, D. A. (2010). *Evaluation for risk of violence in Juveniles*. Oxford University Press.

Jhang, F. H. (2017). Economically disadvantaged adolescents' self-concept and academic achievement as mediators between family cohesion and mental health in Taiwan. *International Journal of Mental Health and Addiction, 15*, 407–422. https://doi.org/10.1007/s11469-017-9737-z

Kamal, C. (2006). *The probation service in Singapore*. 127TH International training course visiting experts' papers, Resource material series, p. 67.

Kingon, Y. S., & O'Sullivan, A. L. (2001). The family as a protective asset in adolescent development. *Journal of Holistic Nursing, 19*(2), 102–126. https://doi.org/10.1177/089801010101900202

Koh, L. L., Day, A., Klettke, B., Daffern, M., & Chu, C. M. (2021). An exploration of risk and protective characteristics of violent youth offenders in Singapore across adolescent developmental stages. *International Journal of Forensic Mental Health, 20*(4), 349–363. https://doi.org/10.1080/14999013.2021.1886203

Lai, V., Zeng, G., & Chu, C. M. (2016). Violent and nonviolent youth offenders: Preliminary evidence on group subtypes. *Youth Violence and Juvenile Justice, 14*(3), 313–329. https://doi.org/10.1177/1541204015615193

Larson, R. W. (2000). Toward a psychology of positive youth development. *American Psychologist, 55*(1), 170–183. https://doi.org/10.1037/0003-066X.55.1.170

Leffert, N., Benson, P. L., Scales, P. C., Sharma, A. R., Drake, D. R., & Blyth, D. A. (1998). Developmental assets: Measurement and prediction of risk behaviors among adolescents. *Applied Developmental Science, 2*(4), 209–230. https://doi.org/10.1207/s1532480xads0204_4

Li, D., Ng, N., Chu, C. M., Oei, A., Chng, G., & Ruby, K. (2021). Child maltreatment and protective assets in the development of internalising and externalising problems: A study of youth offenders. *Journal of Adolescence, 91*, 35–47. https://doi.org/10.1016/j.adolescence.2021.07.002

Lipsey, M. W. (2000). *Effective intervention for serious juvenile offenders*. US Department of Justice, Office of Justice Programs, Office of Juvenile Justice and Delinquency Prevention.

Masten, A. S. (2001). Ordinary magic: Resilience processes in development. *The American Psychologist, 56*(3), 227–238. https://doi.org/10.1037//0003-066x.56.3.227

Masten, A. S. (2021). Resilience of children in disasters: A multisystem perspective. *International Journal of Psychology, 56*(1), 1–11. https://doi.org/10.1002/ijop.12737

Milburn, N. G., Stein, J. A., Lopez, S. A., Hilberg, A. M., Veprinsky, A., Arnold, E. M., ... & Comulada, W. S. (2019). Trauma, family factors and the mental health of homeless adolescents. *Journal of Child & Adolescent Trauma*, 12, 37–47.

Ministry of Social and Family Development. (2022). https://www.msf.gov.sg/policies/Rehabilitation-of-Offenders/Community-based-Rehabilitation/Probation-Order/Probation-Programmes/Pages/Probation-Core-Programmes.aspx

Minuchin, S., Rosman, B. L., Baker, L., & Minuchin, S. (2009). *Psychosomatic families: Anorexia nervosa in context*. Harvard University Press.

Moffitt, T. E. (2017). *Adolescence-limited and life-course-persistent antisocial behavior: A developmental taxonomy* (pp. 69–96). Routledge.

O'Connell, M. E., Boat, T., & Warner, K. E. (2009). *Preventing mental, emotional, and behavioral disorders among young people: Progress and possibilities*. National Academy Press.

Oyserman, D., & Markus, H. R. (1990). Possible selves and delinquency. *Journal of Personality and Social Psychology, 59*(1), 112–125. https://doi.org/10.1037//0022-3514.59.1.112

Reczek, C. (2014). Conducting a multi family member interview study. *Family process, 53*(2), 318–335. https://doi.org/10.1111/famp.12060

Richman, J. M., Rosenfeld, L. B., & Bowen, G. L. (1998). Social support for adolescents at risk of school failure. *Social Work, 43*(4), 309–323. https://doi.org/10.1093/sw/43.4.309

Rijo, D., Brazão, N., Barroso, R., da Silva, D. R., Vagos, P., Vieira, A., Lavado, A., & Macedo, A. M. (2016). Mental health problems in male young offenders in custodial versus community based-programs: Implications for juvenile justice interventions. *Child and Adolescent Psychiatry and Mental Health, 10*, 40.

Rutter, M. (1987). Psychosocial resilience and protective mechanisms. *American Journal of Orthopsychiatry, 57*(3), 316–331. https://doi.org/10.1111/j.1939-0025.1987.tb03541.x

Seidman, E., Chesir-Teran, D., Friedman, J. L., Yoshikawa, H., Allen, L., Roberts, A., & Aber, J. L. (1999). The risk and protective functions of perceived family and peer microsystems among urban adolescents in poverty. *American Journal of Community Psychology, 27*(2), 211–237. https://doi.org/10.1023/A:1022835717964

Sharma, V., Ortiz, M. R., & Sharma, N. (2020). Risk and protective factors for adolescent and young adult mental health within the context of COVID-19: A perspective from Nepal. *The Journal of Adolescent Health, 67*(1), 135–137. https://doi.org/10.1016/j.jadohealth.2020.04.006

Son, C., Hegde, S., Smith, A., Wang, X., & Sasangohar, F. (2020). Effects of COVID-19 on college students' mental health in the United States: Interview survey study. *Journal of Medical Internet Research, 22*(9), e21279. https://doi.org/10.2196/21279

Steinberg, L., Chung, H. L., & Little, M. (2004). Reentry of young offenders from the justice system: A developmental perspective. *Youth Violence and Juvenile Justice, 2*(1), 21. https://doi.org/10.1177/1541204003260045

Steinhausen, H. C., & Metzke, C. W. (2001). Risk, compensatory, vulnerability, and protective factors influencing mental health in adolescence. *Journal of Youth and Adolescence, 30*(3), 259–280. https://doi.org/10.1023/A:1010471210790

Symister, P., & Friend, R. (2003). The influence of social support and problematic support on optimism and depression in chronic illness: a prospective study evaluating self-esteem as a mediator. *Health psychology, 22*(2), 123. https://doi.org/10.1037/0278-6133.22.2.123

Tanaka, M., Wekerle, C., Schmuck, M. L., Paglia-Boak, A., & MAP Research Team. (2011). The linkages among childhood maltreatment, adolescent mental health, and self-compassion in child welfare adolescents. *Child Abuse & Neglect, 35*(10), 887–898. https://doi.org/10.1016/j.chiabu.2011.07.003

Thoits, P. A. (2013). Self, identity, stress, and mental health. In C. S. Aneshensel, J. C. Phelan, & A. Bierman (Eds.), *Handbook of the sociology of mental health* (pp. 357–377). Springer. https://doi.org/10.1007/978-94-007-4276-5_18

Triana, R., Keliat, B. A., & Sulistiowati, N. M. D. (2019). The relationship between self-esteem, family relationships and social support as the protective factors and adolescent mental health. *Humanities & Social Sciences Reviews, 7*(1), 41–47. https://doi.org/10.18510/hssr.2019.715

Van Dijk, M. P., Branje, S., Keijsers, L., Hawk, S. T., Hale, W. W., & Meeus, W. (2014). Self-concept clarity across adolescence: Longitudinal associations with open communication with parents and internalizing symptoms. *Journal of Youth and Adolescence, 43*(11), 1861–1876. https://doi.org/10.1007/s10964-013-0055-x

Wang, P. W., Liu, T. L., Ko, C. H., Lin, H. C., Huang, M. F., Yeh, Y. C., & Yen, C. F. (2014). Association between problematic cellular phone use and suicide: The moderating effect of family function and depression. *Comprehensive psychiatry, 55*(2), 342–348. https://doi.org/10.1016/j.comppsych.2013.09.006

Williams, S. L., & French, D. P. (2011). What are the most effective intervention techniques for changing physical activity self-efficacy and physical activity behaviour—And are they the same? *Health Education Research, 26*(2), 308–322. https://doi.org/10.1093/her/cyr005

World Health Organization. (2021). *Adolescent mental health* [Fact sheet]. https://www.who.int/news-room/fact-sheets/detail/adolescent-mental-health

Yang, H. J., Wu, J. Y., Huang, S. S., Lien, M. H., & Lee, T. S. H. (2014). Perceived discrimination, family functioning, and depressive symptoms among immigrant women in Taiwan. *Archives of women's mental health*, 17, 359–366.

Zhang, D.-J., Wang, J.-L., & Yu, L. (Eds.). (2011). *Methods and implementary strategies on cultivating students' psychological suzhi*. Nova Science Publishers.

Zeleke, W. A. (2013). Psychological adjustment and relational development in Ethiopian adoptees and their families. University of Montana.

Chapter 8
Conclusions and Recommendations

Chi Meng Chu, David P. Farrington, Dongdong Li, and Adam Oei

Contents

This book presents the findings on emotional and behavioural problems (EBPs) from the *Enhancing Positive outcomes in Youth and the Community* (EPYC) study, a large-scale nationwide longitudinal study of young offenders aged 12–19 years in Singapore. The main purpose of the book is to advance knowledge and provide empirical recommendations on dealing with EBPs among these youths. With an in-depth analysis of an Asian sample of young offenders, this book uniquely contributes to the literature and enables cross-cultural comparisons in the future. Given the variations in prevalence rates of EBPs, as well as differences in youth justice policies across jurisdictions, such cross-cultural comparisons could potentially pave the way for more culturally sensitive rehabilitation policies as well as the sharing of best practices across different jurisdictions. The key findings from each chapter are presented in Table 8.1.

C. M. Chu
Ministry of Social and Family Development, National Council of Social Service, Singapore, Singapore

D. P. Farrington
Institute of Criminology, Cambridge University, Cambridge, UK

D. Li (✉) · A. Oei
National Council of Social Service, Singapore, Singapore
e-mail: li_dongdong@ncss.gov.sg

D. Li et al. (eds.), *Emotional and Behavioural Problems of Young Offenders in Singapore*, SpringerBriefs in Criminology,
https://doi.org/10.1007/978-3-031-41702-3_8

Table 8.1 Key findings

Chapter	Key findings
3. Prevalence and comorbidity	A higher proportion of offenders (54.0%) have at least one EBP, relative to non-offenders (35.4%) 1 in 2 of both the offenders and non-offenders had comorbidity Males (50.7%) were more likely than females (38.9%) to meet the clinical threshold for a self-reported EBP Depression was the most central node to co-occur with other EBPs
4. Depression	Depression improves after entering the justice system Personality, violence exposure, and housing status are risk factors for depression Family environment matters most as the protective factor against depression
5. Drug use	Self-reported EBPs and drug use in young offenders decreased over time From wave 1 to wave 3, the proportion of drug-using youths decreased from 51.1% to 16.9%. Similarly, those who reported any emotional problems decreased from 30.3% to 9.5%, while behavioural problems decreased from 54.6% to 15.4% Behavioural problems increased the risk of drug use while emotional problems did not Drug use did not increase the risk of EBPs
6. Re-offending	Re-offending rates in Singaporean young offenders under community supervision are lower than in other countries (Singapore 23.9% vs others 35.0–64.6%) Among these youths with the same Level of Risk, those with EBPs had higher re-offending rates Behavioural problems, but not emotional problems, continue to have incremental validity in predicting re-offending after accounting for Level of Risk
7. Protective factors	EBPs as well as multiple aspects of the external (social relationships) and internal (personal competence) protective factors among young offenders improved over time after entering the justice system Family-related factors (family functioning, parent attachment, home assets) were identified as effective external protective factors that change along with their associated EBPs over time Cooperation and communication and self-efficacy were identified as effective internal protective assets for their EBPs

The main findings and recommendations can be summarised in the following areas: (1) prevalence and comorbidity of EBPs; (2) EBPs, drug use, and re-offending; and (3) risk and protective factors for EBPs.

8.1 Prevalence and Comorbidity of EBPs

Our findings showed that a higher proportion of offenders (54.0%) have at least one EBP relative to non-offenders (35.4%), using self-reported data. Comorbidity of EBPs is common in both our offender and non-offender samples with approximately 1 in 2 (55% of offenders and 49% among non-offenders) self-reporting two or more comorbid conditions. Rates of comorbid emotional or behavioural problems in High-Risk young offenders were even higher, at almost six times those of Low-Risk youths. This is an important finding with implications for practice, as youths with comorbid problems are at higher risk of persistent re-offending, not just during adolescence (McReynolds et al., 2010) but well into their young adult years (Hoeve et al., 2013).

Looking at specific EBPs, depression is more likely to co-occur with other problems such as somatic and anxiety problems and with behavioural problems such as ADHD and conduct problems. Therefore, changes in depression are likely to influence the greatest changes in other EBPs that it is connected to. The importance of depression in our offender and non-offender comorbidity network suggests that it should be a priority to target in any treatment plan. The call then is for practitioners to screen for emotional issues at intake interviews and at frequent intervals using psychometrically validated self-reports. For young offenders, providing ongoing support for their EBPs even after they have completed their sentences is also important. This can include continued treatment or referrals to community touchpoints for them to turn to for their emotional and behavioural problems. This is especially important when these youths are in situations or environments (e.g., high conflict families) that could increase the risk of their emotional and behavioural problems. To this end, interventions which improve family relations and interactions and those that emphasise a shared responsibility of the family contributing to the youth's problems would be beneficial. This recommendation is supported by the large evidence base for family-based interventions for a range of problem behaviours and emotional problems (Hartnett, et al., 2017; Henken et al., 2007; Slesnick & Prestopnik, 2009).

The relatively larger treatment gap in non-offenders means that careful attention needs to be paid as well to the mental well-being of non-offenders. These findings therefore call for increased upstream efforts to increase mental health literacy among educators and parents, to identify early warning signs of EBPs. However, despite the best efforts of parents, teachers, and adults, they may also fail to identify emotional and behavioural problems in the youths themselves. Hence, it is important to also build resilience among youths such as emotional regulation competencies (Compare et al., 2014) as well as to reduce the stigma of seeking help for emotional problems.

While EBPs are a problem in young offenders, they are not insurmountable. Importantly, the initial rates of EBPs decreased over time. From Wave 1 to Wave 3, those who reported any emotional problems decreased from 30.3% to 9.5%, while behavioural problems decreased from 54.6% to 15.4%. To exclude the possibility that this decrease was due to sample attrition, we re-examined the results using 543 participants who had data for all three waves, and a similar pattern of decrease was found. Therefore, the results suggest that young offenders benefitted from rehabilitation in the Singaporean justice system. Rates of drug use and EBPs in our youths decreased as they went through custody or community sentences. This finding is in line with other studies showing that youths in the justice system had reduced substance use after going through substance abuse treatment (Tripodi & Bender, 2011).

One reason could be the structured routine and support services provided by the justice system to young offenders. An unhealthy and chaotic environment might contribute to drug use and EBPs. Therefore, placing these youths in a secure and stable environment might be another reason for their improvement (Lennox et al., 2013). Although the prevalence of EBPs decreased over time, these youths continued to have persistent problems that warrant post-care support upon the completion of their orders. This community support could be undertaken by social service providers that provide counselling and therapeutic services as well as mentorship programmes. This is exceptionally important, especially if these youths lack prosocial peers, which could put them at elevated risk of re-offending.

8.2 EBPs, Drug Use, and Re-offending

Assessing the severity of EBPs is important for drug risk assessment and rehabilitation. In considering how EBPs and drug use are related, our results partially supported the self-medication theory (Khantzian, 1997), that drugs are used to cope with EBPs, albeit a clearly problematic coping strategy. In other words, drugs were used to alleviate or escape from EBPs, but ultimately may contribute to the worsening of drug use or EBPs. Breaking such unhealthy self-medication patterns in drug use requires a comprehensive and individualised approach. One of the key steps is to identify and address the underlying mechanisms that are driving drug use or re-offending.

In our study, we found that behavioural problems, rather than emotional problems, were significant predictors of drug use in young offenders. These findings provide further support for the clear association between behavioural problems and drug use. One possible explanation is that adolescents may use drugs in social settings with their peers. However, youths with only emotional problems may have smaller peer groups, which could limit peer-influenced drug use. Another factor could be that the anxiety and worry commonly associated with emotional problems may deter youths from engaging in risk-taking behaviours like substance use. Our findings are consistent with the notion that there may be a shared underlying cause between behavioural problems and drug use. Both may be influenced by common risk factors such as a propensity for risk-taking, antisocial attitudes, drug-using peers, and familial substance use (Ali et al., 2016; Cleveland et al., 2008).

Similarly, our findings indicated that the presence of EBPs, especially behavioural problems, was associated with increased rates of re-offending. Among young offenders with similar levels of risk, those with EBPs had higher rates of re-offending. Specifically, those with High-Risk and EBP had the highest re-offending rate, while the lowest re-offending rate was seen in those Low-Risk and without EBPs. Additionally, when predicting re-offending, EBPs showed incremental validity beyond the Youth Level of Service/Case Management Inventory (YLS/CMI) Level of Risk. Despite YLS/CMI Level of Risk being a stronger predictor of re-offending, EBPs remained a significant predictor. Overall, EBPs improved the predictive ability of the YLS/CMI, with behavioural problems being the main driver of this improvement rather than emotional problems.

These findings highlighted the importance of screening for EBPs, as our study revealed a high prevalence of EBPs among young offenders. Rates of EBPs varied from 20.8% in Low-Risk to 65.3% in High-Risk youths. Screening is particularly crucial for High-Risk youths as they are more likely to have EBPs. A thorough assessment for EBPs can prevent under-diagnosis, as our study found that four in ten young offenders had self-reported problems but did not have a corresponding EBP diagnosis. This may involve gathering information from various sources, such as the youth, family members, and other relevant professionals, to gain a holistic understanding of the situation. Including comprehensive screening tests enables case workers to conduct a more accurate assessment of the risk and needs among young offenders, ultimately increasing the effectiveness of interventions.

While our research revealed that only behavioural problems directly predicted re-offending and drug use, emotional problems may still have an indirect impact on treatment outcomes. It is thus important to address all EBPs as potential barriers to treatment and integrate them into the treatment plan along with criminogenic needs. Untreated EBPs can hinder the effective rehabilitation of the underlying causes of drug use. Evidence-based approaches to drug prevention emphasise strategies such as motivation for abstinence and coping skills to manage cravings, which require cognitive and social abilities that individuals with EBPs may lack. For instance, drug abusers with ADHD may struggle with their attention span and face challenges in completing treatment (Baweja et al., 2021). Similarly, offenders with emotional problems like anxiety may struggle to respond effectively in group treatment settings. Additionally, individuals with EBPs may encounter difficulties in forming therapeutic relationships, which are essential for effective treatment. As a result, the effectiveness of the rehabilitation programmes may be compromised by unaddressed EBPs, increasing the likelihood of relapse or re-offending. Therefore, it is crucial to have early screening and individualised treatment plans to integrate interventions that target the specific needs and strengths of the youth such as cognitive-behavioural therapy (CBT), motivational interviewing, family therapy, and/or group therapy to address multiple issues simultaneously.

8.3 Risk and Protective Factors for EBPs

While examining the comorbidity of EBPs, we highlighted the importance of depression as the central node of all EBPs. We therefore conducted deeper analyses on depression, and our research revealed a decreasing trend in depression among young offenders. This trend was consistent with the other EBP outcomes, indicating that EBPs improved for those who were under youth justice supervision, despite individual differences in their trajectories. This may suggest that the programmes that these youths participated in during their sentence were effective in improving their EBPs.

The risk factors for depression were personality, violence exposure, and housing status. Neuroticism, a shared personality vulnerability for many mental health disorders, may be prioritised in treatment planning to improve outcomes for multiple co-occurring disorders with fewer treatments required (Sauer-Zavala et al., 2017). Early violence exposure can negatively impact emotional and cognitive development, leading to trauma-related symptoms and disruptions in stress-regulating systems. Prevention methods such as Triple P aimed at reducing early violence exposure, and interventions like trauma-focused cognitive behavioural therapy, targeting violence-related trauma, have been found to be effective in various settings (Lenz & Hollenbaugh, 2015; Nowak & Heinrichs, 2008). The findings also revealed that for young offenders, those residing in public rental housing showed less improvement in depression compared to those living in other housing arrangements. This resulted in a larger disparity in depression severity by Wave 3, despite similar baseline depression severity levels between groups. These findings suggest the need for additional support for young offenders that are from lower socio-economic backgrounds. Support could include increased access to early health and mental health screening services to address depression and related disparities.

Besides risk factors, we also conducted a detailed examination of the protective factors related to depression and the general emotional and behavioural problems (EBPs) among young offenders. Specifically, we identified family functioning, parent attachment, and home assets as external protective factors that were effective in reducing EBPs. Those youths with a strong family environment showed lower levels of EBPs on average. Moreover, those who experienced improvements in these family-related factors over time also showed sharper improvements in EBPs. In addition, the findings indicated that moderate levels of protective factors in the home environment were effective in reducing depressive symptomatology. This suggests that interventions aimed at improving protective factors within the family environment, even if they raise them to a moderate level, may be sufficient in alleviating depression. Thus, increasing protective factors within the family environment should be the focus of interventions, with the goal of achieving at least a moderate level of protection.

While the youths' environment plays an important role in their mental health development, their internal resources and personal competencies contribute as well. Specifically, we found that cooperation and communication and self-efficacy were two effective internal protective factors. Similar to the family-related factors, changes in these competencies were associated with changes in EBPs over time. We also observed unique patterns for two other competencies, namely, problem-solving and self-awareness, which predicted changes in emotional problems but not behavioural problems. These findings highlighted the importance of strength-based interventions that focus on identifying and building on the strengths and capabilities of young offenders. Interventions should be implemented to teach these youths communication and social skills and offer them opportunities to practice such skills. These skills can enable them to establish healthy relationships, resolve conflicts in a non-violent manner, and effectively communicate their needs and emotions to others (Frey et al., 2000). Additionally, by developing problem-solving skills, these youths can learn to identify and address challenges or obstacles in their lives, rather than resorting to negative or impulsive behaviours. As a result, with better communication and problem-solving skills and a positive self-perception, young offenders are more likely to successfully reintegrate back into society (Hodgkinson et al., 2021). They can engage in healthier relationships, effectively manage conflicts, and make responsible choices. Moreover, these skills can enhance their employability, educational opportunities, and overall well-being, reducing their risk of re-offending and thus promoting a positive reintegration process.

8.4 Conclusion

In conclusion, the findings from these analyses confirmed the high prevalence and comorbidity of emotional and behavioural problems when youths entered the justice system. EBPs, especially behavioural problems, contributed significantly to the continued involvement in criminal behaviours such as drug use and re-offending. Nevertheless, an encouraging finding from the present study is that the EBP rates decreased sharply over time, indicating that young offenders benefitted from the rehabilitation programmes in the Singapore justice system. The findings also highlighted the importance of both external and internal protective factors in promoting positive outcomes. The study identified family functioning, parent attachment, and home assets as effective external protective factors, while cooperation and communication, self-efficacy, problem-solving, and self-awareness were identified as effective internal protective factors. These findings underscore the importance of building up environmental and personal competencies in interventions aimed at addressing EBPs among young offenders. Further research and interventions targeting these protective factors have the potential to make a meaningful impact in improving the well-being of these youths and reducing their risk of EBPs in the future.

References

Ali, A., Carré, A., Hassler, C., Spilka, S., Vanier, A., Barry, C., & Berthoz, S. (2016). Risk factors for substances use and misuse among young people in France: What can we learn from the substance use risk profile scale? *Drug and Alcohol Dependence, 163*, 84–91. https://doi.org/10.1016/j.drugalcdep.2016.03.027

Baweja, R., Soutullo, C. A., & Waxmonsky, J. G. (2021). Review of barriers and interventions to promote treatment engagement for pediatric attention deficit hyperactivity disorder care. *World Journal of Psychiatry, 11*(12), 1206–1227. https://doi.org/10.5498/wjp.v11.i12.1206

Cleveland, M. J., Feinberg, M. E., Bontempo, D. E., & Greenberg, M. T. (2008). The role of risk and protective factors in substance use across adolescence. *Journal of Adolescent Health, 43*(2), 157–164. https://doi.org/10.1016/j.jadohealth.2008.01.015

Compare, A., Zarbo, C., Shonin, E., van Gordon, W., & Marconi, C. (2014). Emotional regulation and depression: A potential mediator between heart and mind. *Cardiovascular Psychiatry and Neurology, 2014*, 324374. https://doi.org/10.1155/2014/324374

Frey, K. S., Hirschstein, M. K., & Guzzo, B. A. (2000). Second step: Preventing aggression by promoting social competence. *Journal of Emotional and Behavioral Disorders, 8*(2), 102–112. https://doi.org/10.1177/106342660000800206

Hartnett, D., Carr, A., Hamilton, E., & O'Reilly, G. (2017). The effectiveness of functional family therapy for adolescent behavioral and substance misuse problems: A meta-analysis. *Family Process, 56*(3), 607–619. https://doi.org/10.1111/famp.12256

Henken, H. T., Huibers, M. J., Churchill, R., Restifo, K., & Roelofs, J. (2007). Family therapy for depression. *The Cochrane Database of Systematic Reviews, 2007*(3), CD006728. https://doi.org/10.1002/14651858.CD006728

Hodgkinson, R., Beattie, S., Roberts, R., & Hardy, L. (2021). Psychological resilience interventions to reduce recidivism in young people: A systematic review. *Adolescent Research Review, 6*, 333–357. https://doi.org/10.1007/s40894-020-00138-x

Hoeve, M., McReynolds, L. S., & Wasserman, G. A. (2013). The influence of adolescent psychiatric disorder on young adult recidivism. *Criminal Justice and Behavior, 40*(12), 1368–1382. https://doi.org/10.1177/0093854813488106

Khantzian, E. J. (1997). The self-medication hypothesis of substance use disorders: A reconsideration and recent applications. *Harvard Review of Psychiatry, 4*(5), 231–244. https://doi.org/10.3109/10673229709030550

Lennox, C., Bell, V., O'Malley, K., Shaw, J., & Dolan, M. (2013). A prospective cohort study of the changing mental health needs of adolescents in custody. *BMJ Open, 3*(3), e002358. https://doi.org/10.1136/bmjopen-2012-002358

Lenz, A. S., & Hollenbaugh, K. M. (2015). Meta-analysis of trauma-focused cognitive behavioral therapy for treating PTSD and co-occurring depression among children and adolescents. *Counseling Outcome Research and Evaluation, 6*(1), 18–32. https://doi.org/10.1177/2150137815573790

McReynolds, L. S., Schwalbe, C. S., & Wasserman, G. A. (2010). The contribution of psychiatric disorder to juvenile recidivism. *Criminal Justice and Behavior, 37*(2), 204–216. https://doi.org/10.1177/0093854809354961

Nowak, C., & Heinrichs, N. (2008). A comprehensive meta-analysis of triple P-positive parenting program using hierarchical linear modeling: Effectiveness and moderating variables. *Clinical Child and Family Psychology Review, 11*(3), 114–144. https://doi.org/10.1007/s10567-008-0033-0

Sauer-Zavala, S., Wilner, J. G., & Barlow, D. H. (2017). Addressing neuroticism in psychological treatment. *Personality Disorders: Theory, Research, and Treatment, 8*(3), 191–198. https://doi.org/10.1037/per0000224

Slesnick, N., & Prestopnik, J. L. (2009). Comparison of family therapy outcome with alcohol-abusing, runaway adolescents. *Journal of Marital and Family Therapy, 35*(3), 255–277. https://doi.org/10.1111/j.1752-0606.2009.00121.x

Tripodi, S. J., & Bender, K. (2011). Substance abuse treatment for juvenile offenders: A review of quasi-experimental and experimental research. *Journal of Criminal Justice, 39*(3), 246–252. https://doi.org/10.1016/j.jcrimjus.2011.02.007

Index

D. Li et al. (eds.), *Emotional and Behavioural Problems of Young Offenders in Singapore*, SpringerBriefs in Criminology,
https://doi.org/10.1007/978-3-031-41702-3

MIX
Papier aus verantwortungsvollen Quellen
Paper from responsible sources
FSC® C105338

If you have any concerns about our products,
you can contact us on
ProductSafety@springernature.com

In case Publisher is established outside the EU,
the EU authorized representative is:
Springer Nature Customer Service Center GmbH
Europaplatz 3, 69115 Heidelberg, Germany

Printed by Libri Plureos GmbH
in Hamburg, Germany